107/600

THE
ART OF
COMPETITION

MARK ALLEN: 6X IRONMAN CHAMPION
PHOTOGRAPHY: NICK BORELLI

06	INTRO	
08	CHAPTER **1**:	CHANGE
10	CHAPTER **2**:	PREPARE
46	CHAPTER **3**:	NATURE
48	CHAPTER **4**:	REFLECTION
88	CHAPTER **5**:	FEAR
90	CHAPTER **6**:	ACTION
130	CHAPTER **7**:	STUCK
132	CHAPTER **8**:	ENGAGE
170	CHAPTER **9**:	ART
178	CHAPTER **10**:	REALIZE
216	LIMITED EDITION	
266	EPILOGUE	
270	BIOS	

FOREWORD

Foreword to The Art of Competition
By Jim Collins
© 2014 by Jim Collins

Imagine you're gliding along a vast, glass-smooth ocean. Suddenly a missile breaks through the surface and shoots towards the sky. There is a singular moment when the missile enters your consciousness, as if it all happened in an instant. But of course, the missile had been rising, unseen, for perhaps thousands of feet before it broke the surface—a moment of breakthrough, only after an unseen period of build-up.

Now consider a singular moment, October 14, 1989, at 2:59 PM. Mark Allen and Dave Scott matched each other stride for stride, almost synchronized, having raced for nearly eight hours within a few feet of each other, pounding out a pace that would shatter the Hawaii Ironman course record by nearly twenty minutes, hurtling toward a finish that would be Dave Scott's best day ever in an event he'd won six times. Then, with less than two miles to go in the marathon, still within touching distance of each other, it happened. "Something just said 'Go'," said Allen, "and it was like I was shot out of a cannon. There was no thought, no 'this is the moment,' there was just this thing that said 'Go.'" And so, in the seeming snap of a finger, he broke away to win his first of what would become six Ironman victories in six starts. It looks like an instantaneous moment of breakthrough, but like a missile breaking the surface, Allen's breakaway moment came only after years of rising from below, having been to the Ironman six times prior without a single win. Obscured in the riveting moment at 2:59 PM on October 14, 1989, is the real story, the long cumulative flywheel effect.

Picture a huge heavy flywheel. You want to get the flywheel turning as fast and with as much momentum as possible. You begin to push. You get one slow, creaky turn. But you don't stop; you keep pushing, in an intelligent and consistent direction. You get two turns. You don't stop; you keep pushing. You get four turns, then eight. The momentum begins to build. You keep pushing, turn upon turn, push upon push ... sixteen turns, thirty-two, sixty-four, a hundred, a thousand, ten thousand, and then – bang! – the flywheel hits breakthrough, and just keeps accelerating, building momentum. Greatness never happens in a single moment, but only as the result of cumulative buildup to breakthrough.

When Mark Allen reached out to me to write a foreword for this wonderful creation, The Art of Competition, I asked, "Why me?" I'm not an Ironman competitor. And while I've been to Kona, when my wife Joanne Ernst won the Ironman in the mid-1980s, I've never personally experienced the journey of despair running a marathon in ninety degree heat on black moonscape after swimming and cycling for six hours. "I'd like to see if you can link what I'm trying to convey here with the good-to-great journey you've written about," Mark replied. "I have an instinct that there are connections." I immediately flashed upon one of the key ideas we uncovered in Good to Great: the flywheel effect.

But as I got to know Mark better through our conversations about the book, I came to see a second, even deeper link, one that captures why I felt compelled to write this foreword. Making the leap from great results to enduring greatness, to reach an iconic and visionary stature, requires building upon a set of core principles—core values and a core purpose, a guiding philosophy that you hold to, no matter what—while also stimulating change, improvement, innovation and renewal in pursuit of BHAGs (Big Hairy Audacious Goals). In our great company research, we call this "Preserve the Core / Stimulate Progress": keep the core values, yet change the practices and methods; stay true to core purpose, yet adjust strategy based on conditions; hold fast to principles, yet embrace new technologies that change the game. At the core of Mark's racing ethic was a simple purpose: To run my best race. "Sometimes that might be good enough to finish first, sometimes not," he said. "But I need to know—with searing self-honesty—that I could not have raced any stronger, no matter what anybody else thinks, no matter how bad I feel, no matter what place I finish."

I expected to see much of Mark's text dedicated to the famous 1989 race with Dave Scott, seen by many as greatest in Ironman history, with Mark winning by less than a minute in a race that lasted more than eight hours. But delightfully he spends more text on 1995, which Mark considers to be his greatest race. "After the 1995 race, nearly every top competitor came up to me and said, 'I would have just given up, and resigned myself to the fact that winning the race was impossible,'" reflected Mark, "I'd come off the bike thirteen and half minutes behind the race leader." It's one thing to stay focused, to be unrelenting, when you're leading the race with Dave Scott and have a clear chance to win. It's another when you're miles back in fifth place, thirty-seven years old, feeling vulnerable, when giving up would be both understandable and unseen. And then add in that his competitors had made a pact before the race to compete against him as a group, trading off responsibility to push him to the limit in the swim and bike, in hopes of destroying his will before the marathon. Without his strong inner core, he might well have capitulated; Mark's 1995 race flowed not from cheering crowds, but from inner character and constancy of purpose.

Greatness is an inherently dynamic process, not an end point; the moment you think of yourself as great, your slide toward mediocrity will have already begun. Mark exemplified this philosophy, not letting what everyone else felt was his greatest race – the 1989 Ironman – define and imprison him. Mark just kept turning the flywheel, kept getting better, kept living the core and stimulating progress. 1989 might have been a perfect competition for the world to see, but 1995 was an exquisite work of art because it most tested and best expressed his inner core.

I resonate with this core, in what I like to call the quest for "fallure" (pronounced fall-yer) over "failure." I've been a rock climber for more than 40 years, and I've come to see climbing—like Mark's approach to racing—as an inner journey, not one of conquering the rock, but of conquering myself. There can come a moment of self-doubt on an at-your-limit sport climb. Forearms fill with lactic acid, draining fingers of their grip power. Heart-rate spikes. Breathing becomes rapid and shallow. Saliva thickens with the metallic taste of adrenaline and fear. You are looking at the next section of rock, uncertain if the holds are good enough to hang from while you clip into protection.

FOREWORD

You have a limited amount of time before your body gives out ... minutes, or maybe only seconds ... tick, tick, tick. Uncertainty, fear, and pain accumulate to the point of decision: failure or fallure? You can "let go" and let the rope take your weight, giving-up without really trying. That is failure. Fallure, on the other hand, means that you still might fall, but you do not let go. You give a 100% committed effort to go up, and if you fall, you know – and only you know – that you could not have tried any harder. Personal-best moments come when climbing right into the fallure zone, when fingers might explode off the holds at any moment, yet somehow you hang on to the top of the climb. Ah, that is perfection!

When I asked Mark to tell me the story behind this book, he said: "I'd been asked for years about my approach to racing and competition, but I could never quite find the words to capture the essence of it. There was something indefinable," he continued, "something I felt, but could not convey in a traditional essay, and certainly not in any training manual." Mark then related how, on a visit to Japan, the quotes that grace these pages just began pouring out, like seeds that had been gestating for years suddenly sprouting up through the earth.

Then he had a spectacular idea: blend these poetic quotes with nature. Indeed, this book could just as easily been titled The Nature of Competition, as Mark sees nature as a super-recharging station for creativity and competitive drive. He brings this notion to life in Chapter 9, telling the story of his trip to Alaska just weeks prior to the 1995 race, where he exchanged his aerobic training regimen for a connection with grand external landscapes and inner contemplation, to restore cells so depleted that blood-work revealed levels more like someone in his sixties than his thirties. He continues with how he then surrendered to the stark beauty of the Big Island, plugging into it as a recharging station during the 1995 race, summoning the will to persist. It's not so much about spending an excessive amount of time outside; it's about paying attention–pausing to be drenched by a sunset orange, cocking an ear to the chattering of happy birds, noting the slosh-smack sounds of water on a shore, or marveling at how that October Moon got so big. Mark's book is a reminder to be more fully present when blessed with an exquisite or magnificent moment. Plug in. Pause. Recharge. Go.

The great photographer Ansel Adams described his moment of creative breakthrough, his making of the famous 1927 photograph titled Monolith, of the Northwest Face of Half Dome: "I had achieved my first true visualization! I had been able to realize a desired image: not the way the subject appeared in reality, but the way it felt to me." That is the artistic gift, the ability to see– or perhaps "sense" – something others cannot quite put their finger on, and use art to express it. And that is what Mark has done here, capturing the inner terrain of the true competitor, through photographs and quote-poems, unlike anything I have seen before. The Art of Competition shows that while Mark Allen's competitive races might rest in the past, his creative journey continues. And as with any true artist, the journey never ends.

Jim Collins
Boulder, Colorado
July 2013

DEDICATION:
THIS BOOK IS DEDICATED TO THE WORK AND INSPIRATION OF BRANT SECUNDA WHOSE INFLUENCE WAS THE FUEL THAT SPARKED ITS WRITING, AND WITHOUT WHOM I WOULD NOT HAVE THESE STORIES TO TELL.

INTRODUCTION

In 1968 I received my first dose of athletic inspiration as I watched the Mexico City Olympics from my home near San Francisco. For two solid weeks the world's best summer sport athletes competed on a very visible stage, as ABC Wide World of Sports brought us the unfolding drama in everything from track and field to gymnastics to swimming. Each night Jim McKay hosted sport at its best and provided depth to the human beings behind this athletic greatness. Their sheer physical capabilities mesmerized me, and the clear strength of determination the victors showed was astounding.

Champions where honored with coveted Olympic medals while those who faltered went home with nothing more than memories. What made the difference between the two? What inner drive or training or strategy gave the best their edge? What transformed a strong showing into a winning competitive performance that can only be described as art, defined not by paint strokes but by swim strokes, not by static statues but by bodies hurling through time and space, eventually coming to rest with a salute to the judges.

Is competitive prowess innate, or can anyone willing to dedicate their life to it learn some hidden secret that will make them the best?

Our genetics only vary about one half of one percent between all people on the planet. This means we are all 99.5% exactly the same. So how does one person, or a team of individuals, extract that and so much more from such an insignificant difference in makeup? What separates challenger from champion? Which far corner of one's personality unleashes that superhuman potential to rise above impossible odds and slay the dragon? Is it fate? Destiny? Good luck? Or is there a way that we mere mortals can call upon something innate that changes the game and tilts the scales in our favor during the moments that count most?

I did not find out answers to these questions until twenty years later, during one of the greatest duels of all time against a seemingly invincible competitor, in an event called "the toughest one-day sporting event in the world." It was in 1989 at the Ironman Triathlon World Championship in Hawaii that I got my first taste of what the Art of Competition is and how all of my years of "competing" were never going to allow me to discover this elusive yet potent mindset that changes the impossible into the attainable. I'll tell that story in detail later in the book, but first I want to give you a sense of what this expansive, powerful state of being is.

The Art of Competition is when a physical, visceral experience—filled with sweat and pain, with extreme control and pure gut-wrenching strength—transforms into a flow of movement where every single cell inside the body is working in unison faster than the brain can possibly coordinate. There is scientific research that has measured this uniquely expanded yet indefinable state where, for lack of a better way to describe it, a person's energetic body takes over and thought becomes secondary. The normal boundaries that distinguish every cell, muscle fiber and tendon disappear. The athlete's body stops wasting time processing thoughts about trying to go fast, to hold on, or to stay calm. It just does all that is necessary to deliver the goods without hesitation. The usual way this is described is that you are "in the flow," a state where time slows so you can anticipate the ball or where eternities pass in the blink of an eye and pain becomes background static, where you stop thinking about victory or failure and just become a vehicle for a truly great performance. This is when competition is transformed into art.

Many gifted athletes can have incredible performances without ever experiencing the Art of Competition simply because they are rich with natural talent. But there always comes a day when it's do or die, where they must go beyond their born-with endowments because an uncooperative opponent is not following that seemingly superior athlete's competitive strategy. Failure is looming. Without walking across that tightrope separating competition from art, truly great victories will be elusive.

Your greatest moments might be just inches beyond your reach until you cross that precipice, one where fear beckons from the left and doubt from the right. Mastering the Art of Competition will, however, widen that precarious rope to a step, then a bridge, and suddenly the path becomes so wide that there is no way you can fall off it. A personal best, a world championship, a victory over a supreme opponent will become not only attainable but unavoidable, but you won't really care because you will have achieved something more lasting and fulfilling than any comparative assessment of greatness. You will have achieved The Art of Competition.

The pages that follow will provide you with ways of looking at competition differently than you ever have in the past. The majority of the quotes are words that, if digested slowly, can provide the nutrients necessary to discover this exquisite state for yourself, regardless of whether you are a weekend warrior running through neighborhood alleys and parks in your hometown or a world class athlete calling up excellence while under the very public microscope of televised competition.

Each quote was discovered and cold-steel forged in the heat of Ironman competition. It's the type of competitive dynamic that tests both skill and will, where the intensity of the day ferrets out even the smallest weakness and exposes it with all its rough edges and unsightliness. Champions don't take it personally. They know it's necessary to bring out something lurking even deeper, something better. That thing is greatness. When the all-too-familiar voice that only you can hear starts eroding your resolve with doubt instead of fortifying it with determination, champions gather their forces and step into an unshakable state called the Art of Competition, a place inside were limits are forgotten, uncertainty disappears, where silence takes hold and suddenly there is no room for anything other than possibility.

I invite you to use the words and images in the pages that follow to change your approach and forge athletics into something greater and more enduring than just a race, a meet, or a game. The Art of Competition: it's what we all look for when we watch sports firsthand, and what we all hope to achieve when we take part in them.

CHAPTER 1: CHANGE

The Art of Competition is a call to achieve your greatest dreams and provide you with new ways to focus on them. It may require making some fundamental changes in your approach to sport, to business, to life. The shifts in perspective that will take you from struggling, to comfortable, and then to brilliance are the same for all three. They provide a viewpoint that creates art through your efforts, where excellence and personal perfection will be the only possibilities and deep satisfaction the end result.

It all starts with a dream, an image or a thought that inspires you to take the first step toward something great. The journey from there is rarely predictable. Many times we do reach our ultimate goal, but occasionally we don't. And even when we do, it often takes longer than we had hoped. But hope we must, as this is the fuel that propels us forward even in moments of doubt. Fulfilling dreams is rarely a nice, tidy process and certainly there may be a few rough edges to our character that make the road bumpier than need be. It's these parts of your inner character that the Art of Competition will smooth and transform. Strengths you already have will be heightened. You'll be creating new background hardware to guide your thoughts and actions. All of this can require change. Are you ready? It takes practice to utilize silence rather than mercurial self-talk to pull you through the moments when keeping going no longer seems possible. Learning how to progress from wanting control over your competition to simply embracing the situation with all its challenge and unlikely chaos isn't learned in a one-day crash course. Mastering the ability to regroup, then relaunch with more effectiveness and renewed strength takes practice.

How does change come about? Do we just say "I will change" and voilà, you are a different person without your old habits? Rarely. Changing that which does not work is usually like dying a small death. Procrastination, impatience, overeating, under-sleeping, being fearful, negative or doubtful—whatever it is that you want to change requires a commitment that always tests your reservoir of resolve.

The familiar, even if not effective, is so easy to slip back into! I know this personally and want to share a simple story of a small change that took forever to bring about.

I have a shed where I store some of my most valuable, and of course, oversized items—my sporting gear. I have enough bikes to outfit a team and a quiver of surfboards that will work on every sized wave from small to tall. This treasure trove is guarded by a deadbolt that a few months ago had an internal tumbler that slipped out of place and made the lock impossible to open. I managed to get the deadbolt unlocked one last time and then it was time for CHANGE! Instead of using the same lock that I had for ten years, I now had to use the lock on the doorknob itself. This seems like a very simple change. Right? Here is how it went.

WEEK ONE:

Every single time I went to unlock my shed, I put the key into the deadbolt (old pattern). It was not until I tried to turn the lock that I would immediately realize that, oops, I put the key in the old lock, but needed to use the doorknob lock instead.

WEEK TWO:

Things got a little better. I still put the key in the deadbolt, but remembered this was not the right action BEFORE I turned it to no avail.

WEEK THREE:
I found myself splitting the unlocking process between actually putting the key in the correct lock first and then, yes, still putting it into the wrong one other days. Tough to teach old dogs new tricks, I suppose.

WEEK FOUR:
It was about 75/25 with 75 being the percentage of times that I got it right. Close, but still not the complete cigar.

WEEK FIVE:
I only saw the key go into the old lock once, even though I will admit I started to reach for it a couple of times before I caught myself.

WEEK SIX:
Finally success! No false starts. I put the key in the right lock first time, every time. It took what seemed like an eternity for this simple change to become my new go-to behavior. I have on occasion still reached for the wrong lock, but each time caught myself before the key came in contact with it.

So I pose the question to you: If a simple thing like using a different lock on the same door was so tough, how will the big, and certainly more important, patterns ever get changed? Well, maybe we need to be more vigorous in helping ourselves avoid the wrong lock (the old patterns) in the first place. In my case, I could have put a piece of tape across the old lock as a stern reminder: "Don't go there."

What will be your piece of "tape" put across the pattern that you are trying to change in your pursuit of the art of competition, in changing old ineffective patterns into new ones that take you further in life? What will remind you that you have once again reached for the "old lock," rather than opening the door to your future with the right one? My lock didn't turn, so it was a very quick and clear reminder that I was still in the process of changing an old behavior that no longer served me. I had more work to do until the new effective action became second nature, my go-to action.

I needed to get into that shed just about every day, and with the old lock I had no choice but to change the pattern. I couldn't give up. It took me six weeks, but I finally succeeded. What will force you to keep working on change until it indeed comes about, until you also reach for the right lock to open your storehouse filled with good fortune and joy?

Creating art through athletics, creating something that is a reflection of your personal perfection, takes time. It's made possible by embracing the countless steps it requires to bring it into form, by calling up the patience needed to address each and every challenge along the way, and to have the willingness to change the parts of your internal landscape that could talk you into abandoning your efforts. You might be a rare and lucky one who can make those changes with the flick of a switch. But if you are like most of us who don't get it in an instant, it's certainly worth taking the time to move closer and closer with each opportunity to new go-to behaviors that eventually reveal your priceless gifts. Competition that is true art is created one workout at a time. It is eventually revealed in its entirety, in all its precision, by an athlete who may not be the most gifted, but who has embraced the changes necessary to reveal greatness, the one who stuck with it until that long sought-after goal was reached and art was the result.

CHAPTER 2: PREPARE

PERFECTION DEMANDS...

THE ART OF COMPETITION

13

THE ART OF COMPETITION

14

| EXCELLENCE IS NOT A
| PART TIME JOB.

A CHAMPION EXPLOITS EVERY DETAIL
WITHOUT EVER FORGETTING THE BASICS.

17

OVER PREPARE
    AND UNDER TRAIN.

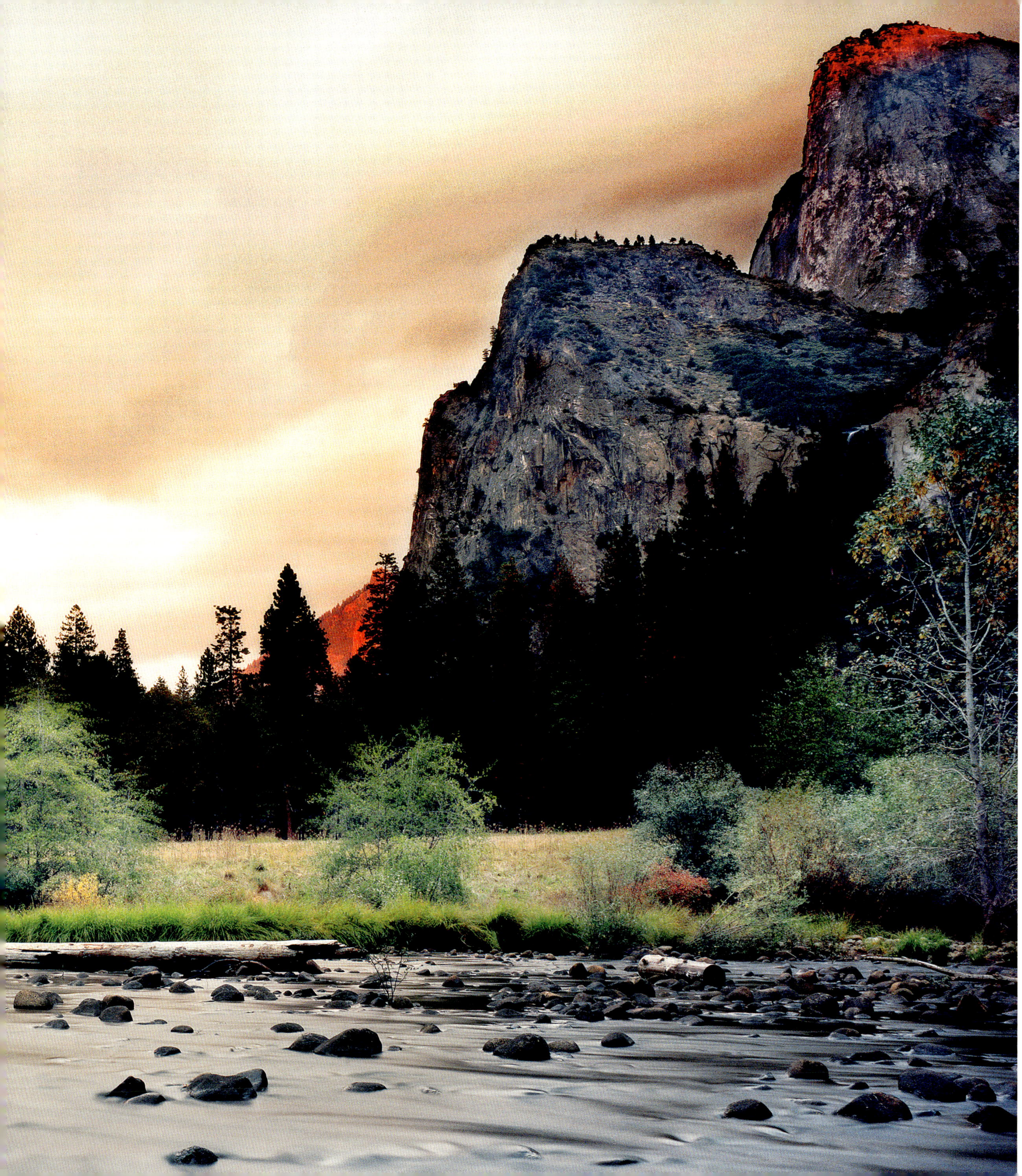

SELF-CONFIDENCE ELUDES
THOSE WHO NEVER FACE FEAR.

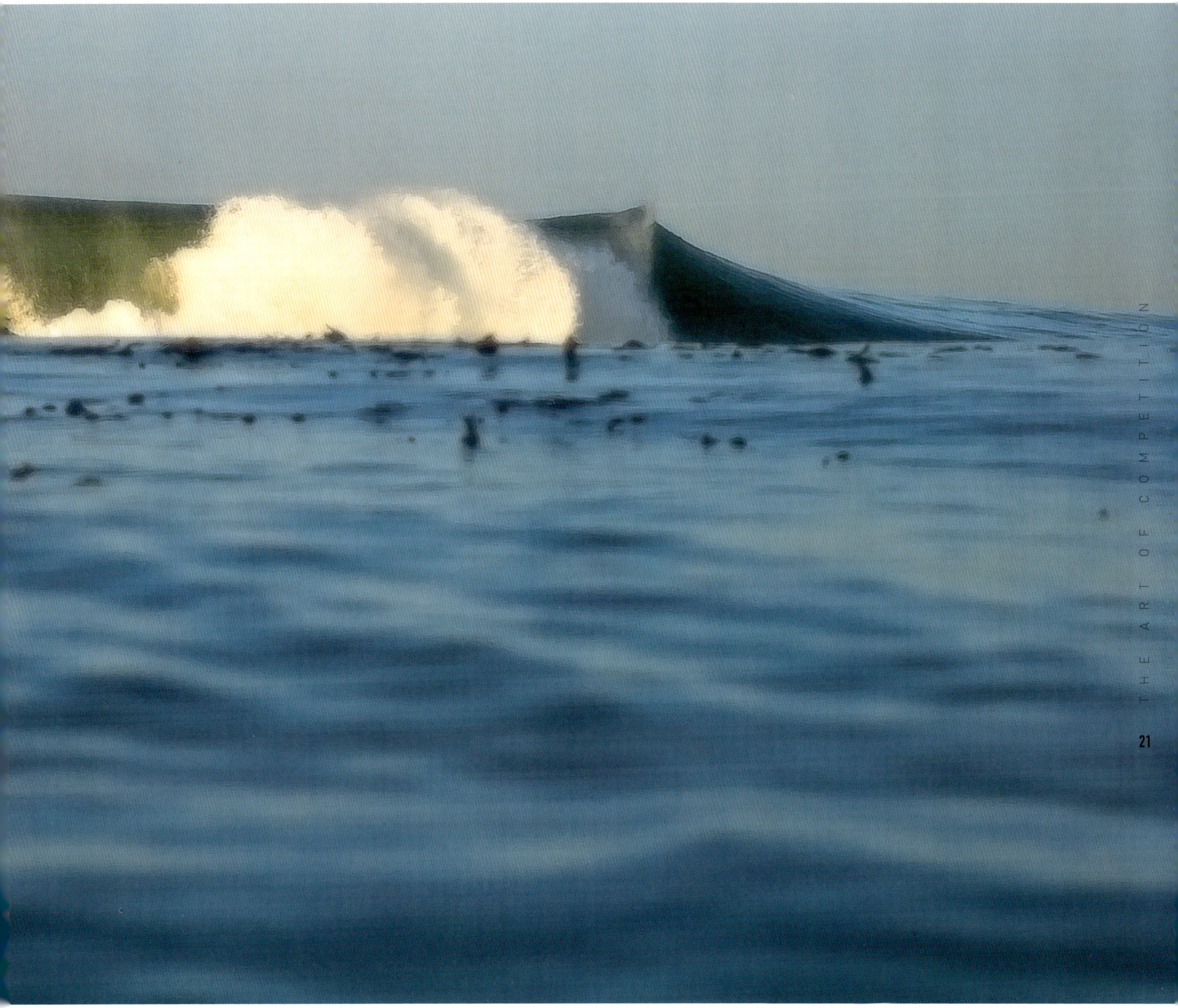

TRAIN TO PERFORM TEN PERCENT BETTER
THAN YOU THINK VICTORY WILL REQUIRE.
ONLY THEN CAN YOU OUT PACE
THE REAL WORLD CHALLENGES.

THE ART OF COMPETITION

23

THE ART OF COMPETITION

24

| WEAKNESS GERMINATES ONLY IF IGNORED.

THE REAL WORLD DOESN'T CARE ABOUT YOUR IDEAL STRATEGY; IT IS BEGGING YOU TO FOLLOW ITS PLAN.

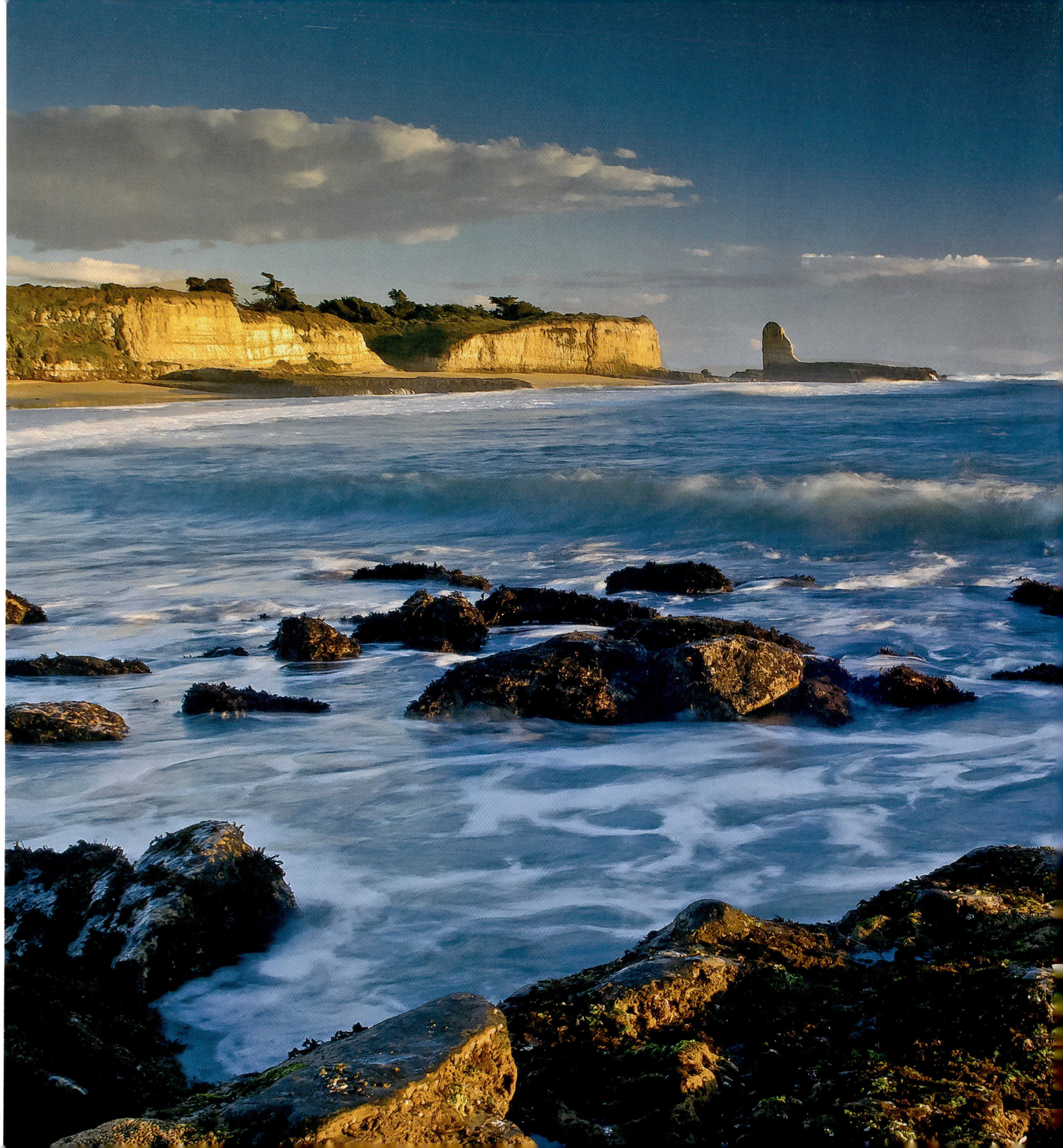

VICTORY IS NOT MEASURED BY NUMBERS IN A LOGBOOK.

THE ART OF COMPETITION

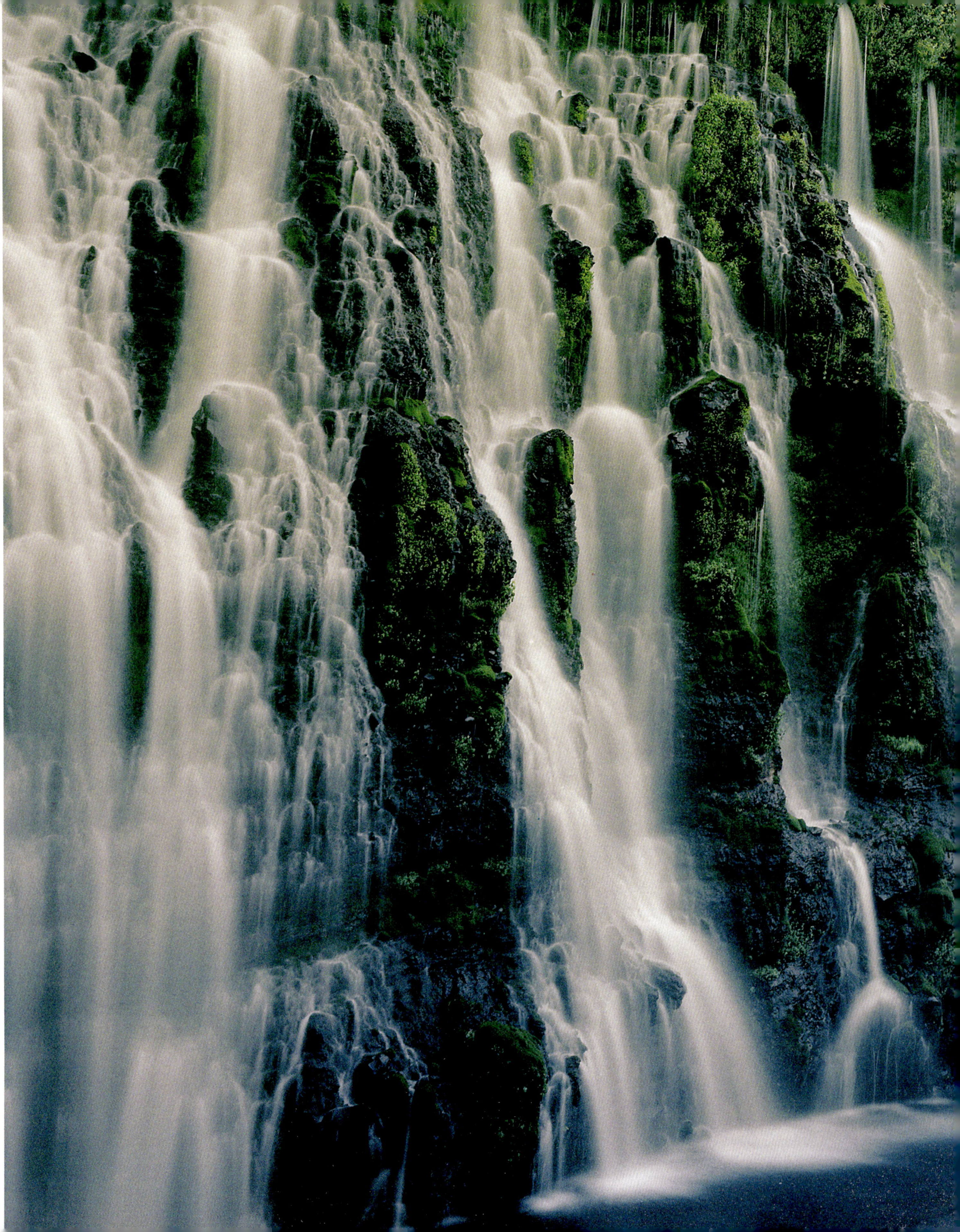

BEATING AN OPPONENT AT THEIR GAME IS TOUGH; BEATING THEM AT YOURS IS NOT.

THE ART OF COMPETITION

EASY CHANGES RARELY LEAD TO VICTORY.

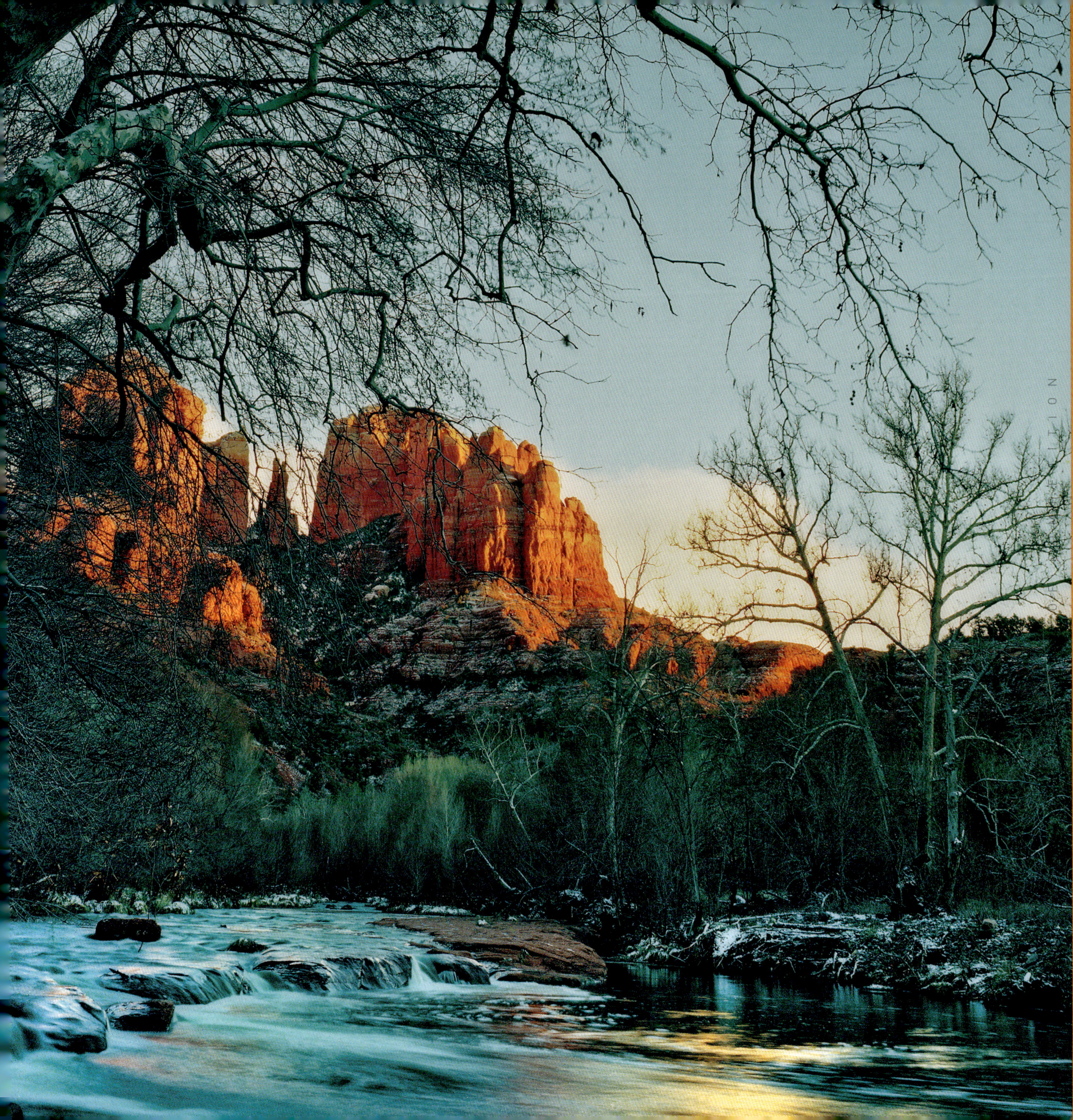

SAVE YOUR BEST FOR THE CONTEST.

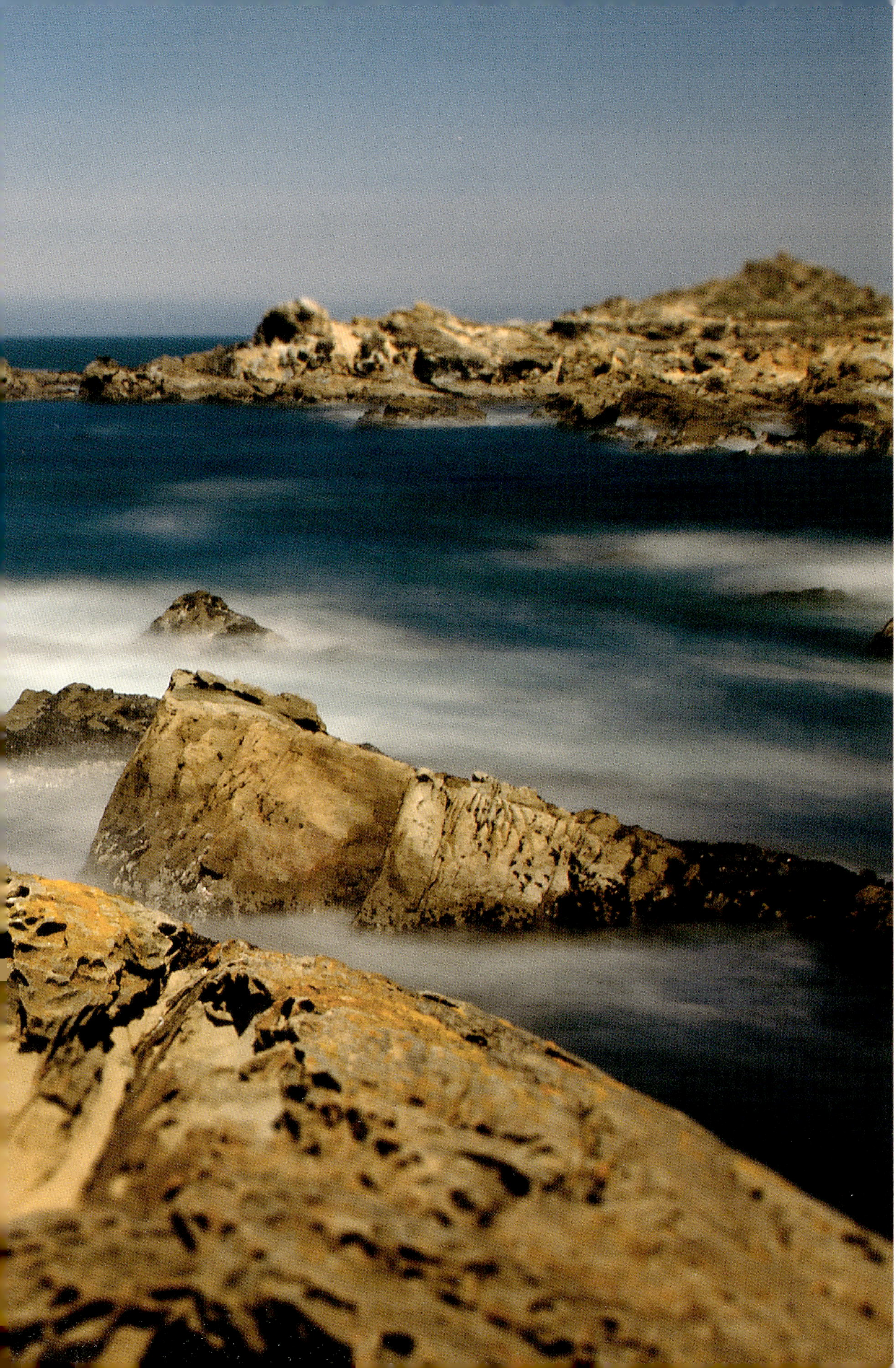

THE ART OF COMPETITION

36

A CHAMPION NEVER LETS NATURAL TALENT GET IN THE WAY OF HARD WORK.

THE ART OF COMPETITION

DISCIPLINE IS FLEXIBLE.

THE ART OF COMPETITION

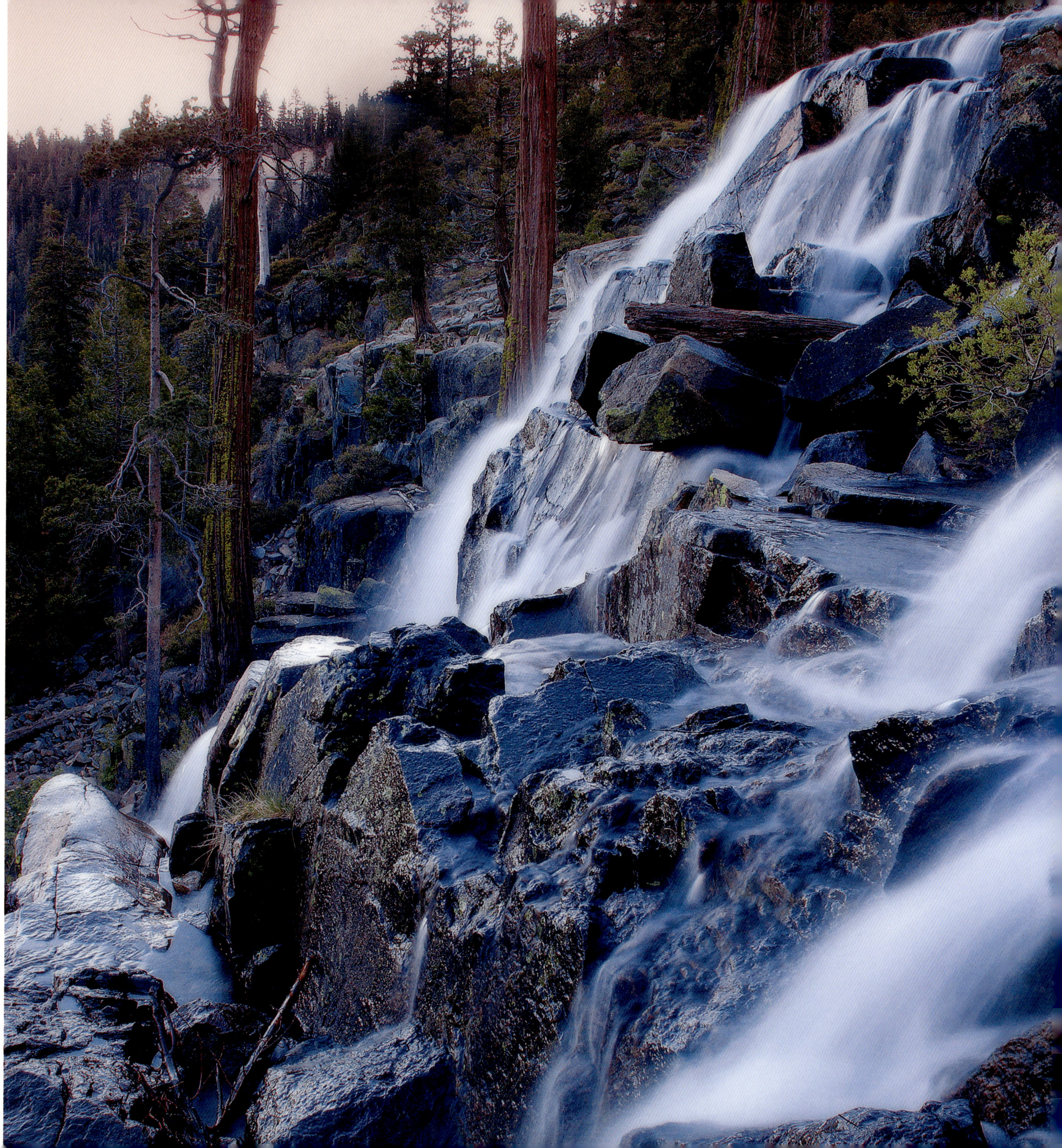

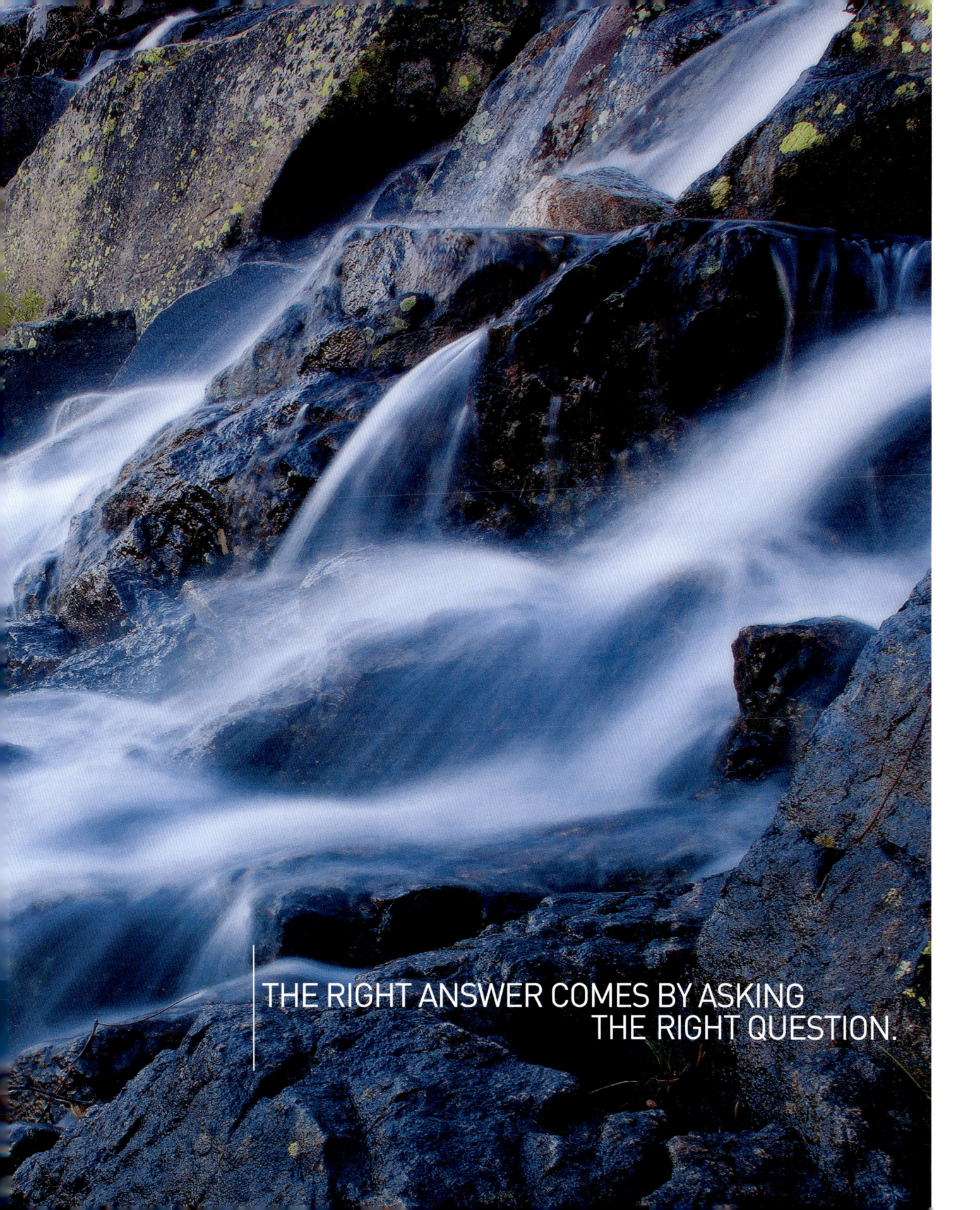

THE RIGHT ANSWER COMES BY ASKING THE RIGHT QUESTION.

LET OTHERS MASTER THE KNOWLEDGE OF YOUR SPORT. A CHAMPION ONLY NEED MASTER ITS APPLICATION.

THE ART OF COMPETITION

43

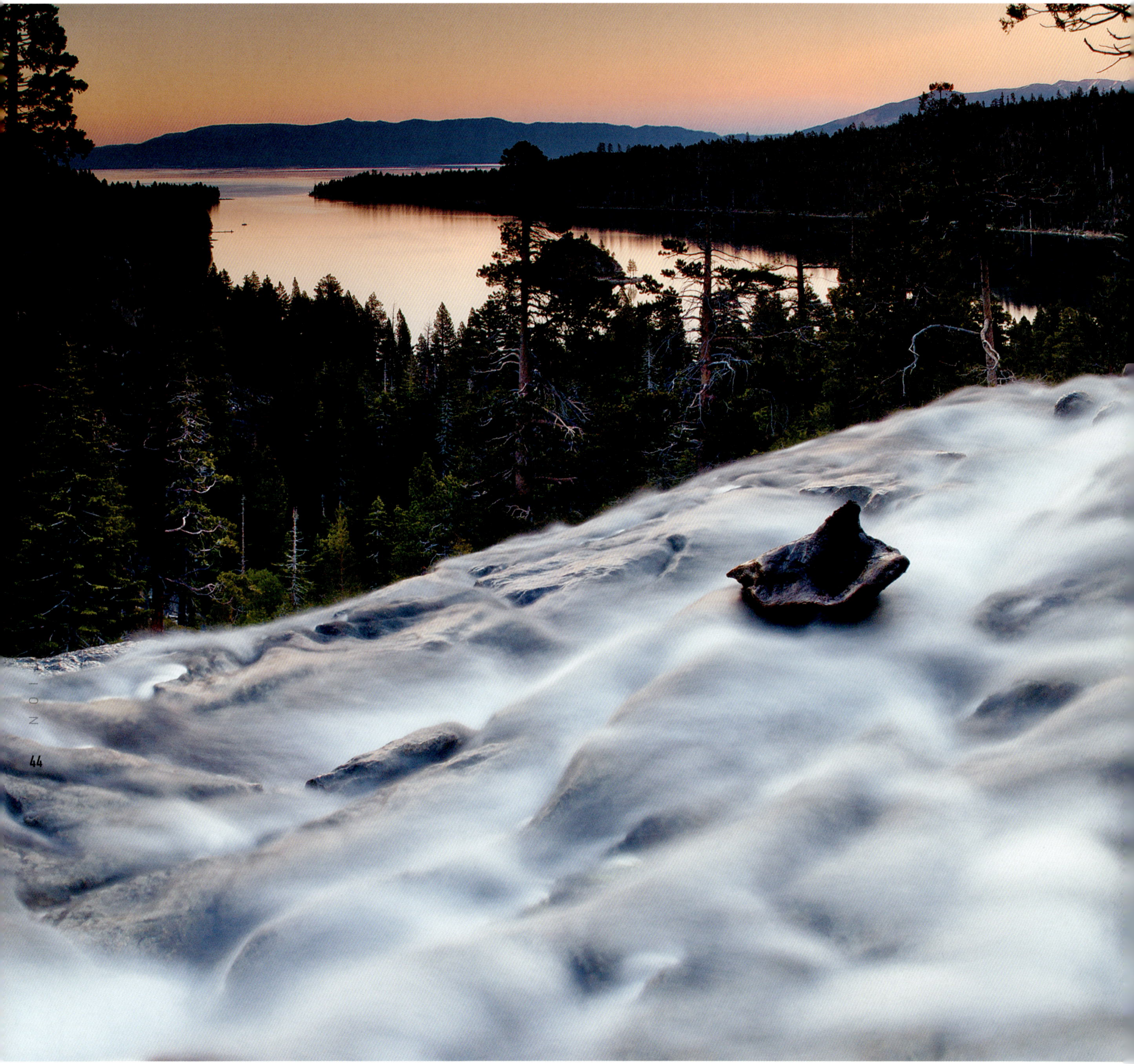

UNCERTAINTY IS THE TEST OF TRUST;
BECOME COMFORTABLE WITH IT.

CHAPTER 3: NATURE

Athletes practice their craft endlessly, perfecting every skill and movement, uncovering their hidden flaws, then preparing some more. But these are usually the tangibles where improvements can be measured. A faster time or better score are the quantifiable pats on the back signaling that, yes, the goal is closer. This is the outer stuff that is bread and butter for most who compete.

But what often gets neglected is parsing out time and energy to hew and shape the inner hardware of your character that must also be activated and sculpted to achieve personal excellence. It's finding your go-to location deep inside that is impervious to impossibility, then using it as a last holdout against the weight of potential failure.

It's learning to use steadiness and calm to overcome insurmountable odds and uncertainty. It's a place inside you that says something like, who cares if this doesn't turn out the way I had hoped? I'm going to give it everything I have anyway!

Now, you may be saying to yourself, "This all sounds great, but I've never been there, and I have no idea if I ever will. My current go-to place is not one that is pretty, and it never answers with the help I need when called upon in critical moments. How can I unlock that which I've never known and haven't the slightest clue how I'm going to find it?"

Fortunately the answer is simpler than you might think! It requires doing something that I am sure you have experienced many times in your life. It's waiting patiently for you to remember it. You've been there before. It's calling your return. It's outside. Its name is Nature!

There was a time when our ancestors lived every day in harmony with nature's rhythms, read each of its subtle signs and found solace in its beauty. Today most of us must make a special effort to come in contact with the precious pockets of nature still thriving. Once there we become overwhelmed with its majesty. Places of pure nature remain so stupendous, no human can ignore its sway on how we feel when we are in its embrace.

Where were you when you felt nature's surge override all your problems, disappointments, challenges or setbacks?

Was it deep in a forest where sound was muted and life's mystery was revealed? Perhaps it was standing looking up at mountain peaks whose names you didn't know, but whose presence became intoxicating. Maybe it was simply a time in your backyard, lost in the bright crimson and burnt ginger colors of the sunset.

We are hardwired to feel good and think positively about life when we gaze silently at the beauty and presence of nature. Limits are forgotten. Doubts disappear. Greatness washes over us and through us. For those moments the whole of life feels like a delicate work of art. Possibility becomes our ally; trust, our closest friend. Placing ourselves in nature is like putting a key in a lock and turning it gently, then peering beyond into something great and deep that cannot be contained in words. Yet it is so familiar that it reflects back to us the depth and greatness of our own character. Remember these moments. Seek them out. They instill the same mixture of limitless possibility and absolute humility that will bring out your personal brilliance. It's the same blend of calm and ultimate trust that turns the key and activates the half-percent difference in genetic makeup between you and your competition, the difference between you being "good" and doing something enduring and perfect that is truly art.

Unfortunately, most of us don't have the time or the means to travel to the far reaches of the earth in search of the masterpieces nature has built. But you can use the photographic images throughout this book to inspire the same passion and focus. Really look at them. What are the words being expressed to you through their splendor? Which part of your potential gets triggered when you gaze into their lasting beauty? Feel the connection between silence and greatness in their colorful radiance. Then, when you can, spend time outside in places that inspire your heart. An inspired heart carries you one step past wanting to quit and fuels your efforts with magnificence.

Shaman Brant Secunda, who you will hear more about later, offers that modern day life has rendered us forgetful of fostering this connection, yet it is so valuable to each of us. He has explained to me so many times how connecting with nature relates to excellence in sports and in life. He emphasized that the best way to ready yourself for any tough challenge is to make sure you are charged up with good energy and a positive outlook, and that the most normal, simple, universally understood way to do that for every human being on the planet is to take a few moments away from the ordinary routine and just experience a slice of nature. He emphasizes that the process is simple, but that the effect can be profound. It could be listening to the sound of a creek or the ocean. It might be watching a sunrise or sunset and just soaking in the colors. Maybe it's simply feeling the earth alive beneath your feet. Brant says this is what fortifies us from the inside out, and with that, great endeavors are possible.

The photos that you are seeing in this book will help you experience that fantastic shift from feeling ordinary to truly being touched by the extraordinary. They are for you. They will help take you beyond the quantifiable and into the immeasurable by allowing qualities like ease and grace, trust and surrender, awareness and assurance to be at your command. Those assets don't fit on a spreadsheet. Passion doesn't come in a package. Having them in your toolbox on game day can lead you to an outlook on competition that is equally implausible or indefinable, take you to a performance that is as lasting as nature's beauty. Start developing them today, through the quotes you are reading, through these wondrous images from nature that are at the core of our world.

CHAPTER 4: REFLECTION

THE ART OF COMPETITION

50

CHALLENGE

Challenge is just a misunderstanding you have about the work your dream is asking you to do to achieve it. Once you agree within yourself to do what it takes, challenge disappears and inspiration takes over.

DREAM

A Dream is the beginning of anything great or meaningful in life.
With dreams we have purpose, and life is worth living.

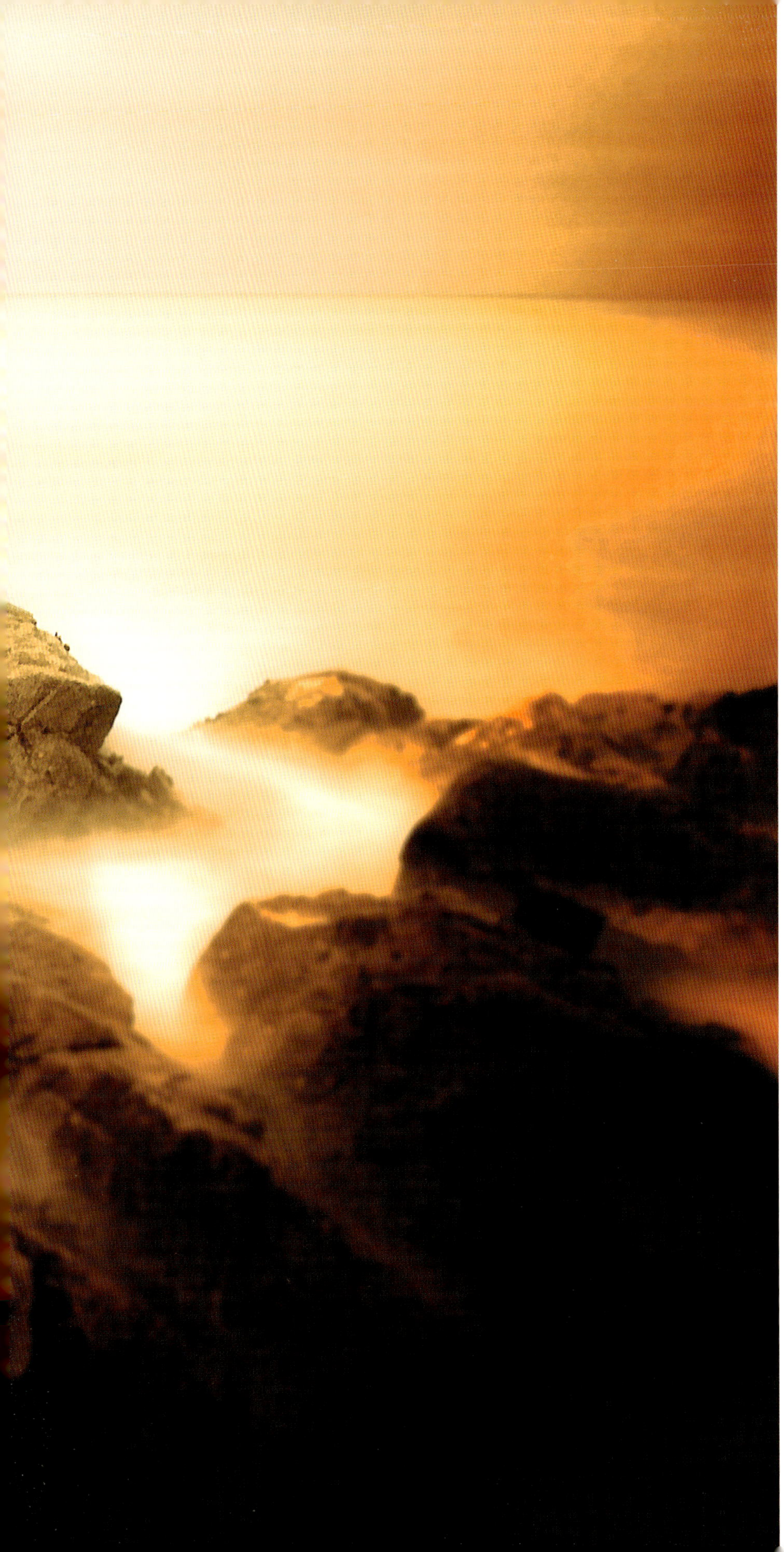

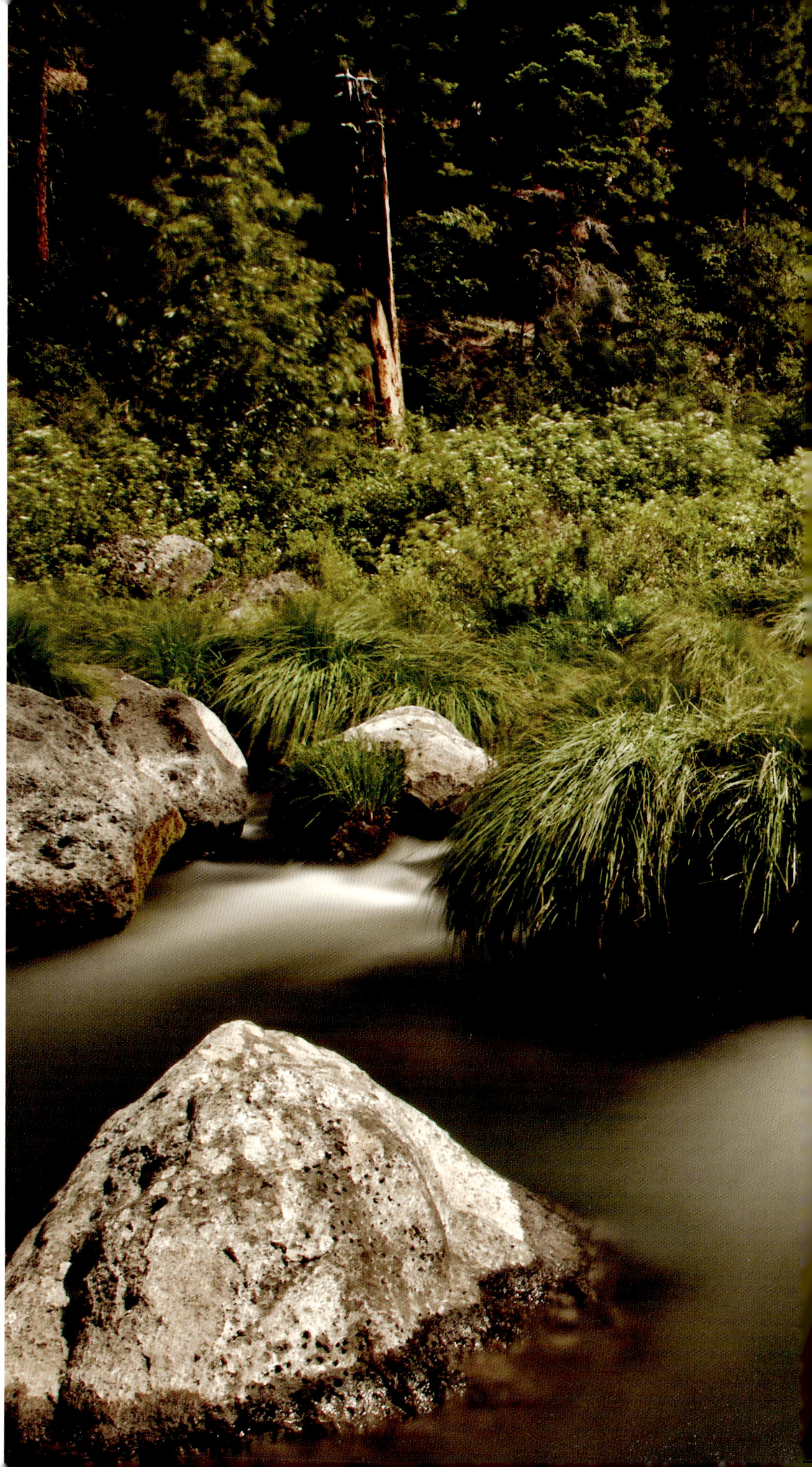

DEFEAT

Defeat is just a temporary moment
where a deep lesson about life can be learned.

RIVAL

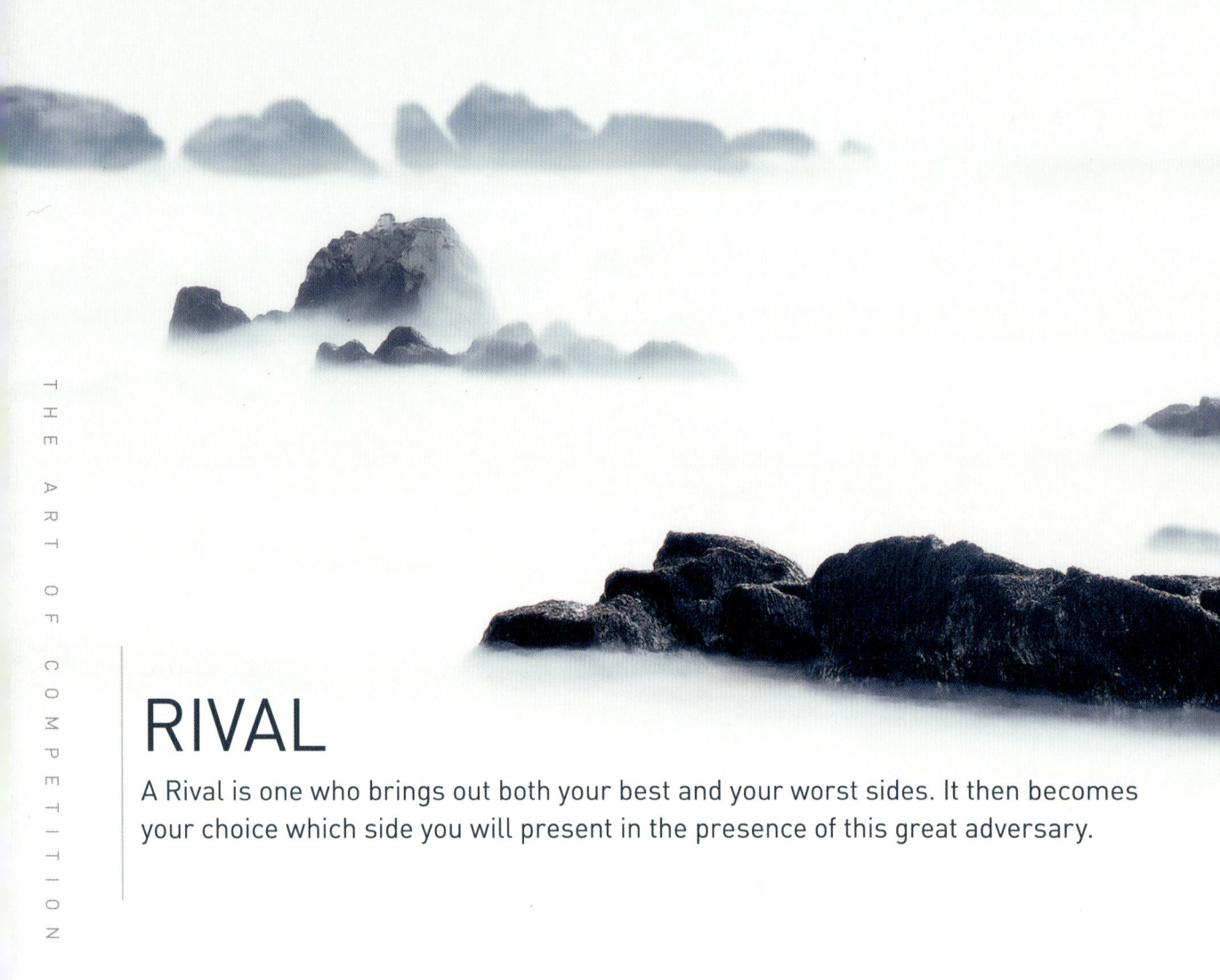

A Rival is one who brings out both your best and your worst sides. It then becomes your choice which side you will present in the presence of this great adversary.

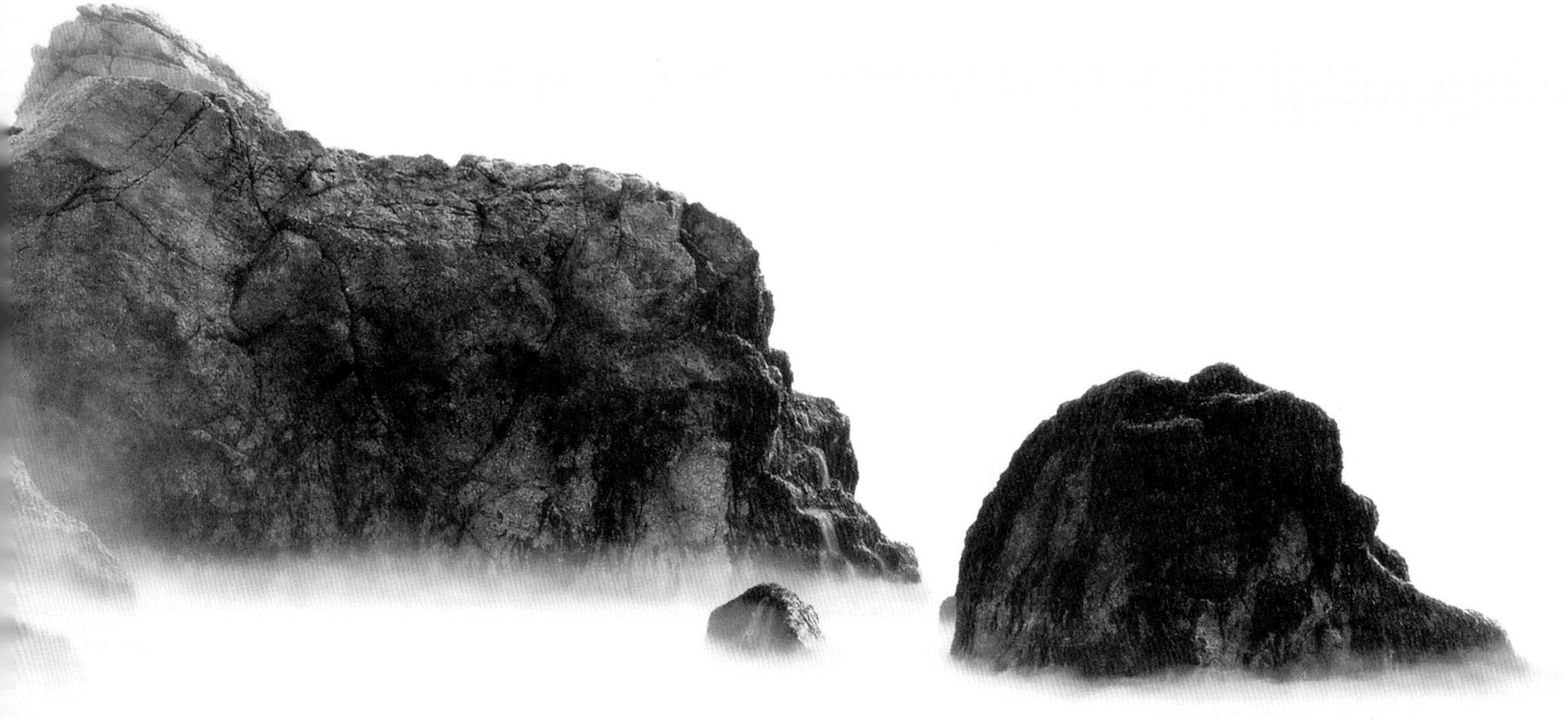

STUCK

Being Stuck has two faces. One can reflect that your current path is wrong and must be abandoned. The other is a reminder that all greatness comes by persevering even if the moment at hand feels hopeless. You must then decide which is the one to follow.

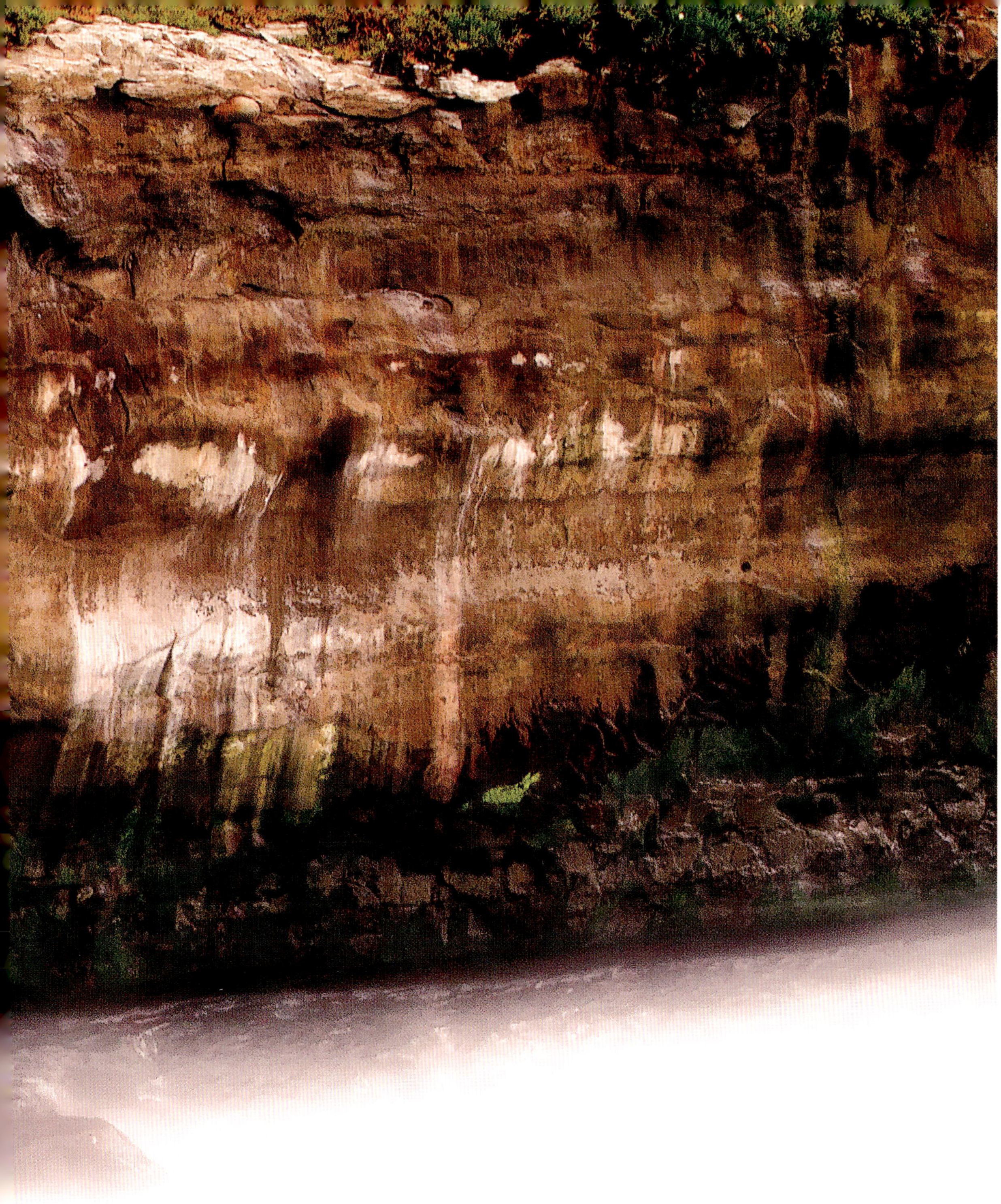

THE ART OF COMPETITION

UNEASINESS

Uneasiness can be a simple case of fear testing your commitment to take the next step. It can also be your inner wisdom picking up subtle warnings against proceeding down a road that is not right.

THE ART

JEALOUSLY

Jealousy strips a person of gratitude.
And without gratitude no amount of greatness
will ever bring fulfillment.

COURAGE

Courage is faith in the unknown. And you might ask if it is possible to truly live without that faith.

65

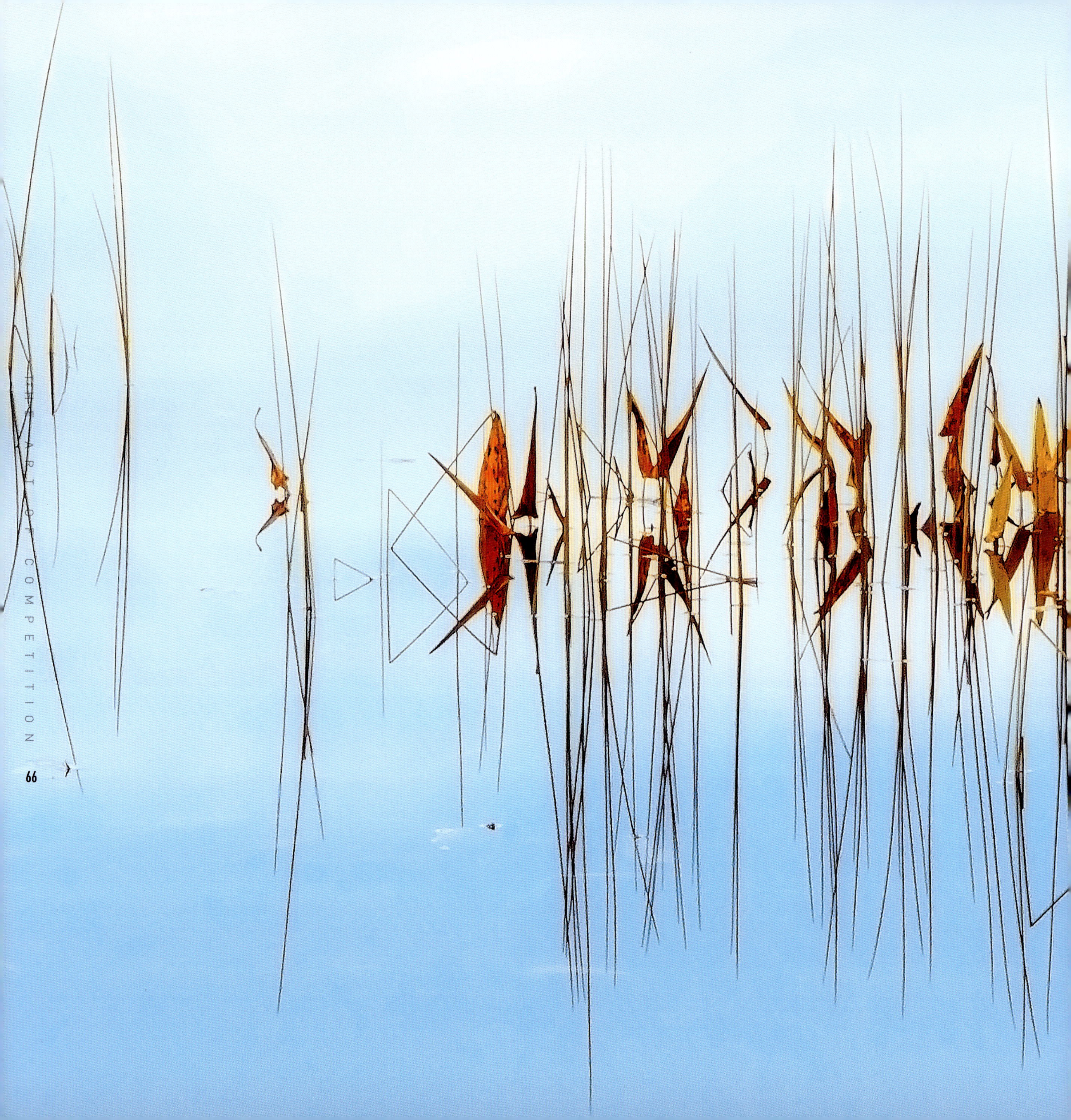

FORGIVENESS

Forgiveness brings new life.
It brings fresh energy like the birth
of new awareness.

SELF-PITY

Self-Pity, if quick and passing, can be like a soft rain that washes away disappointment. But if it lingers it drowns the roots of life.

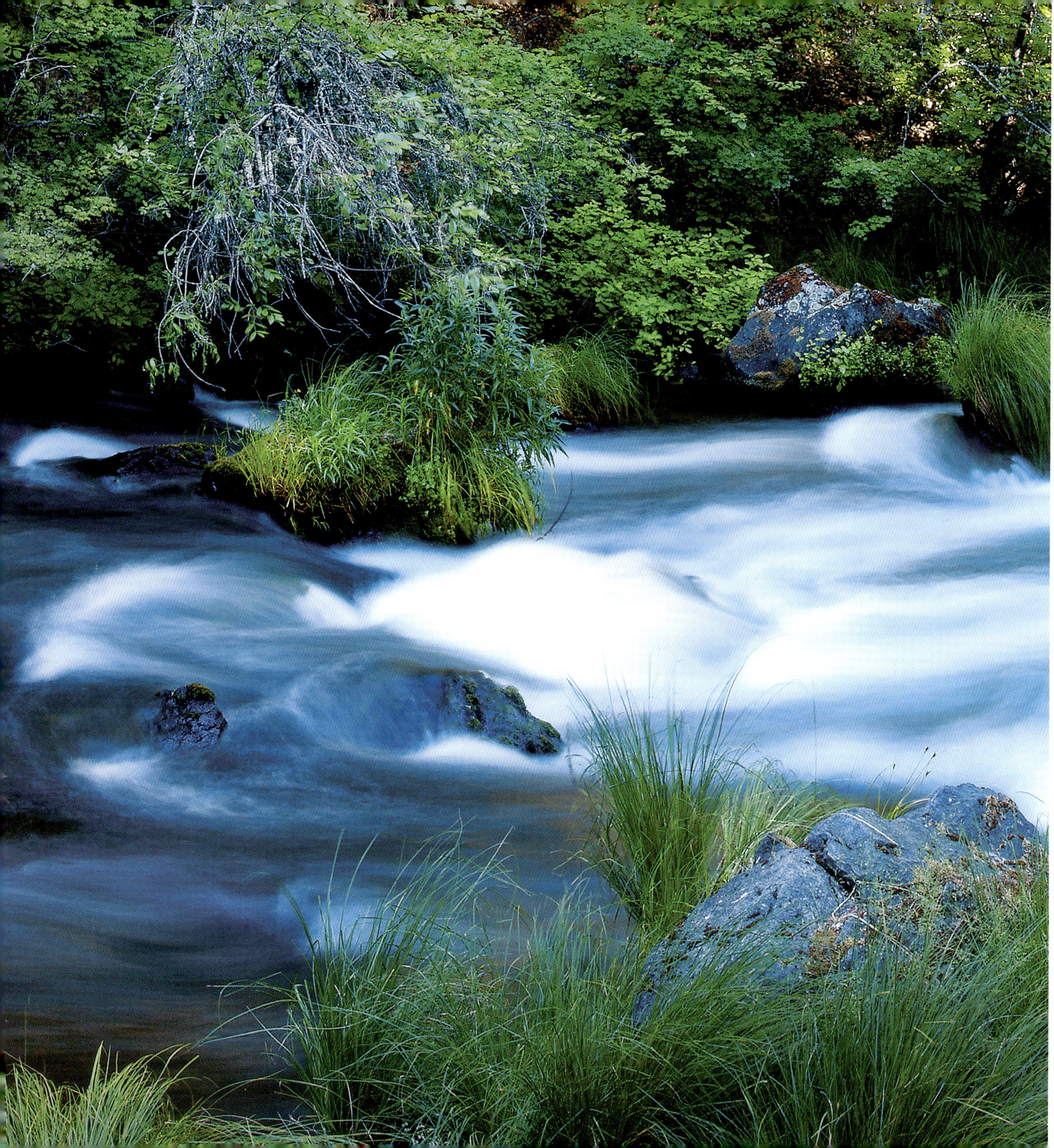

INDECISION

The cloud of Indecision grows when none of the options before you feel right in your heart. Take time until the right decision reveals itself. It may even be present now, but you are afraid to embrace the impact it will have on your life.

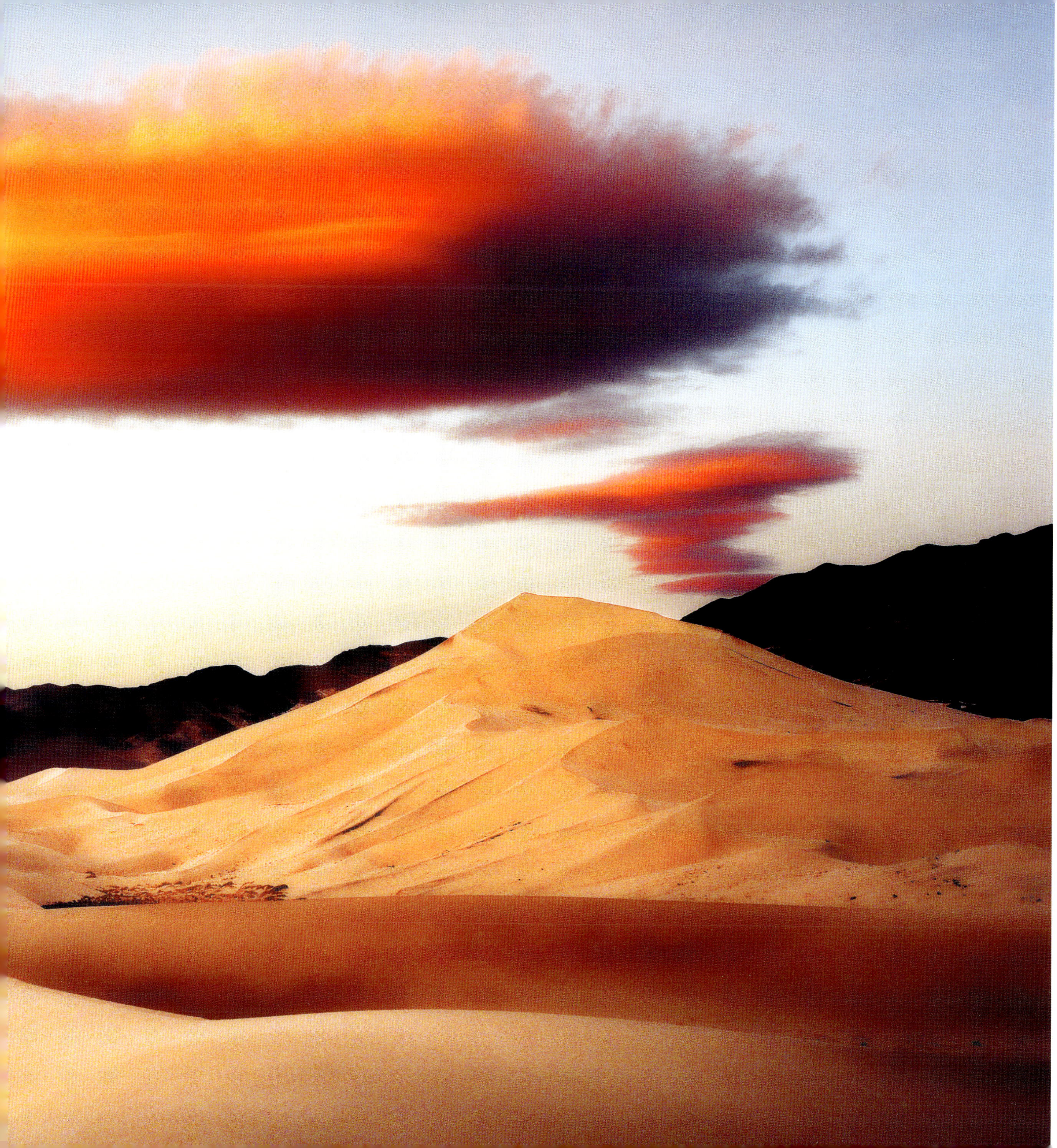

EMPTY FEELING

Empty Feeling comes from the shortsightedness that makes the immediate moment seem like it turned out wrong. With the passing of time, though, you can see that every moment is turning out exactly as it needs to. Fill up with that confidence!

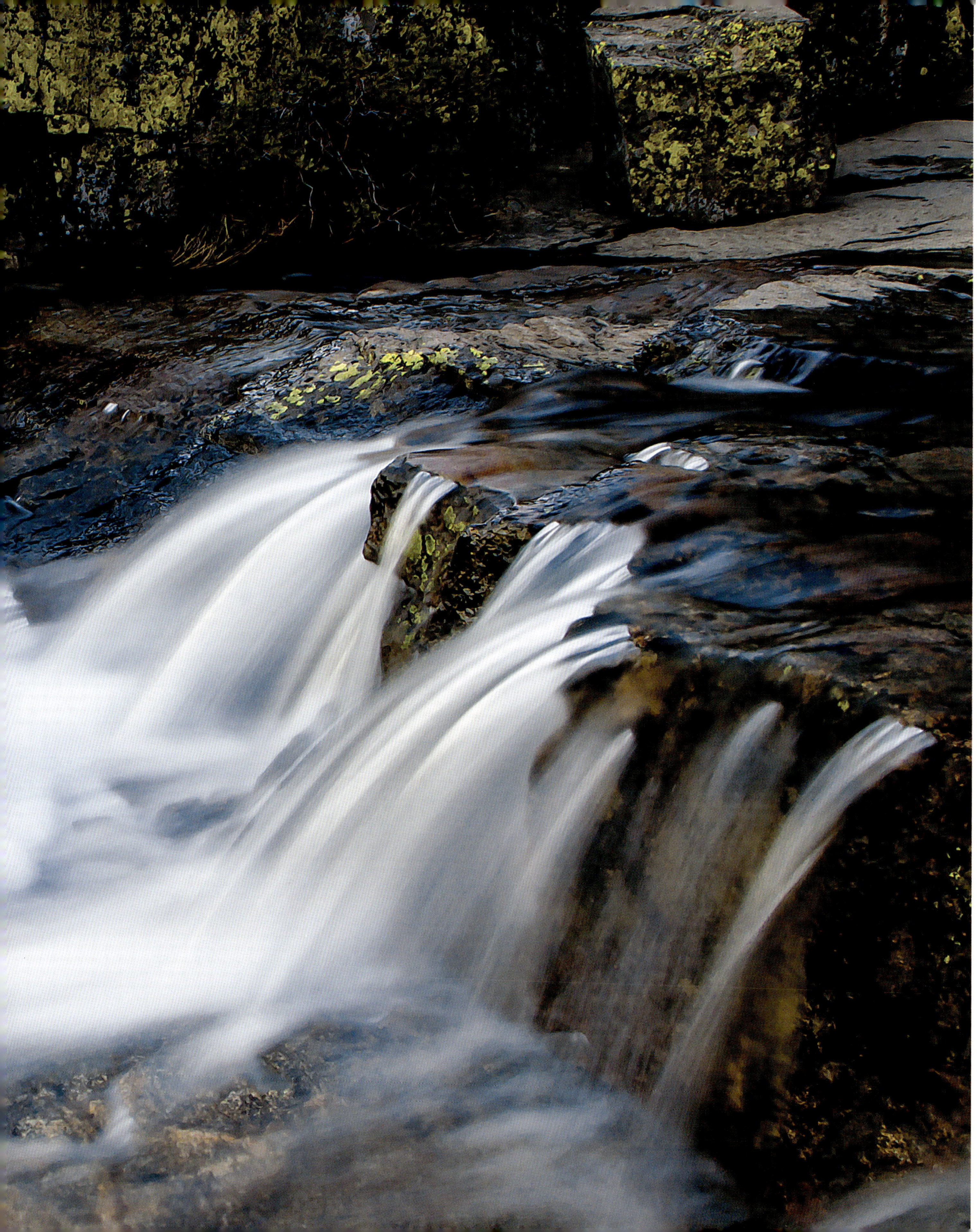

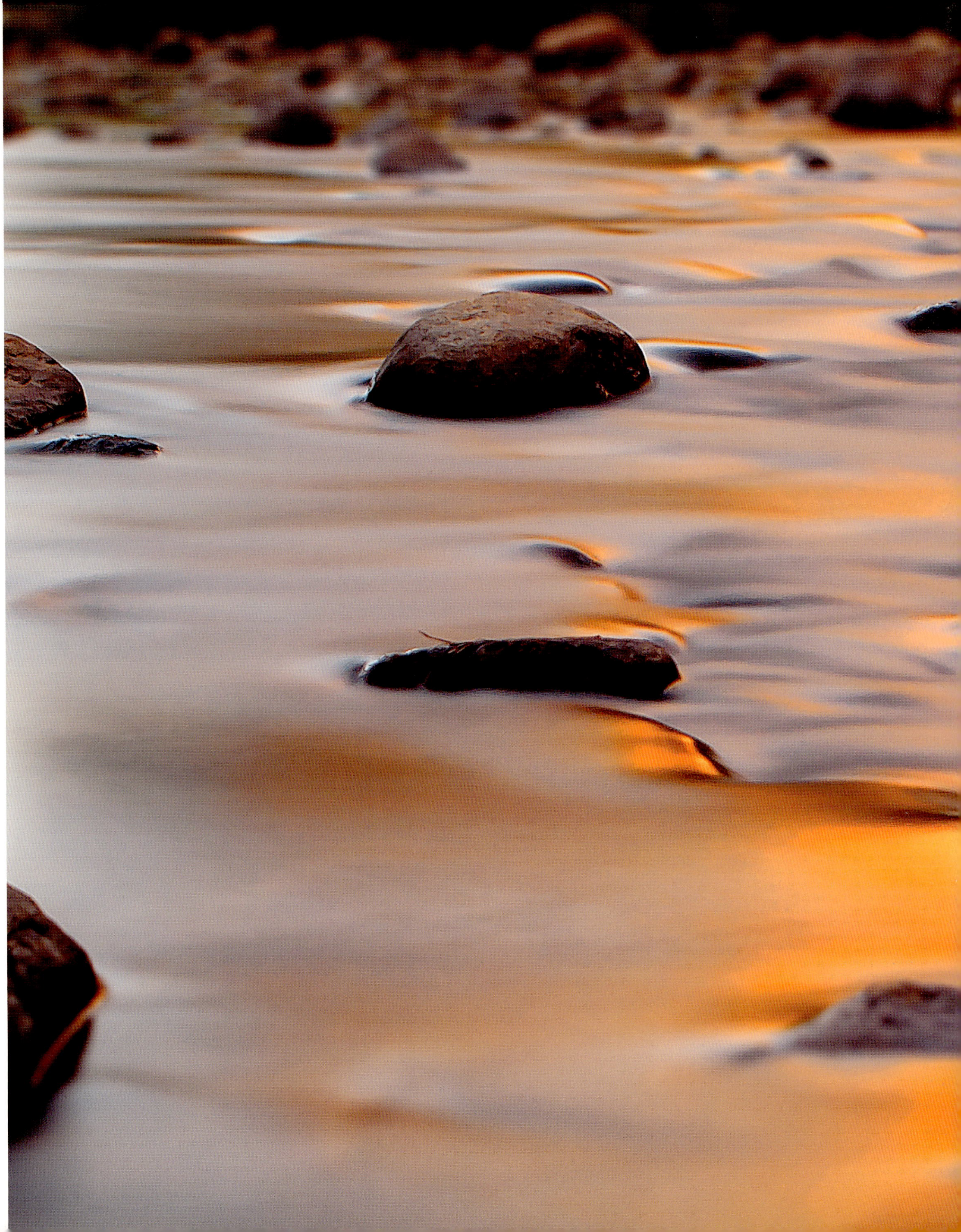

TRAUMA

Trauma is simply an event born out of a calling from the deepest recesses of your being that something is needed that has yet to be embraced.

THE ART OF COMPETITION

76

GIVING UP

Giving Up is turning your back on possibility before you finish sculpting it into the perfect form your vision saw it to be when you embarked on the journey.

THE ART OF COMPETITION

BEING ALONE

Being Alone brings your true nature to the surface.

THE ART OF COMPETITION

79

THE ART OF COMPETITION

80

CALMNESS

Look for Calmness within first. Once you find it there, look around and you will see it everywhere.

MENTAL CONFLICT

Your inner wisdom always knows what is right to do.
Mental Conflict arises when you fear the impact of living that truth.

THE ART OF COMPETITION

ENVIRONMENT

The most important Environment is your internal landscape. Look deeply until you see its beauty and wonder. There you will find the force that inspires the world.

THE ART OF COMPETITION

85

THE ART OF COMPETITION

86

GRATITUDE

The ultimate Gratitude is to be thankful that you are alive. When you find this, then all that may have stood in your way of happiness melts away.

CHAPTER 5: FEAR

Have you ever been afraid? What happens? Do you hold back, maybe just for an instant, or possibly forever? Did you ever regret it later that you let fear get in the way? Fear is part of each of us; we have it to ensure self-preservation. But it's also one of life's greatest teachers, and we must learn to move past it if living fully is our purpose and our goal.

I learned a life lesson about fear in one sentence spoken a number of years ago by an unlikely source. It came from a guy named Walter, who is the brother of my dear friend Lisa. Walter is a surfer by passion, and on any given day is as good as the world's best. We met one November at Lisa's (and of course, Walter's) childhood home on the North Shore of Oahu, the Mecca of surfing. It's the Olympic arena of that sport, and a place anyone worth their board shorts has to journey to at least once in their lifetime. I've surfed since the mid-70s, so for me this was a chance to become one of a select few who has paddled into some of the most perfect and powerful waves in the world.

Walter and I were ready. The swell was big even by Hawaiian standards. Then he uttered the words of warning that paralyzed me. "Whatever you do, don't hesitate at the top of the wave or you're cooked."

"Don't hesitate." It means don't let fear get in the way. What Walter was saying, certainly from experience, is that as you paddle for one of these moving football fields lurching up out of the ocean's depths, no two exactly the same, there will come the moment where you have to apply all the force your body can muster to create enough downward pitch on your board to start the drop into this gigantic moving wall of water. If you hesitate you'll get hung up at the very top of the wave, but just for a moment because in the next instant you will become one with the lip of the wave and get pitched into God's thin air.

Enjoy the ride because at some point you will, with the accelerating force of gravity, come in contact with cement-hard water at the bottom of the wave. Then it's a Mack truck of crushing water spilling over you, turning your useless body into a rag doll with absolutely no control of your destiny for what will seem like an eternity. So have fun!

Walter easily slipped into the first elevator drop that came our way. The next one was mine. All those Ironman championships must count for something, right? I was positioned perfectly. The second wave of the set was coming right to me. I turned toward shore and started to paddle. Up I rose as the first two thirds of the monster passed underneath me. The lip was next. I had to get enough forward speed to start sliding down the face of the wave before the lip pitched. And then...I hesitated.

The world stopped. Walter's words were like a shell going off in my head. "Don't hesitate." In my races I never hesitated. Regardless of how impossible something seemed I still went for it.

I never, ever gave up for one second. Fear was there, but it was always background noise. Yet there I was, a legendary moment was unfolding, and I was hesitating. I had good reason to! It was the biggest, fastest moving wall of water I had ever encountered, and Walter was gone. There was no one in the vicinity to help me if this didn't turn out the way I hoped. It was the wave, my fear and me. If I hesitated a nanosecond longer, one of two things would happen. Either I would miss the wave as it passed underneath me, or I would have my personal Niagara Falls barrel ride without the barrel.

What do you do when fear strikes? Do you hesitate? Does the energy and possibility of the moment pass you by? Do you get pitched into the oblivion of self-doubt wondering if you will ever surface? Or do you just dig with all your might and thrust yourself into life's moving wall of unpredictable waters?

I dug. And dug. And in the next instant I had it! I popped to my feet and dropped into one of creation's most amazing beasts. For the duration of that ride, and then some, I was charged with the moment that exists beyond fear. We've all experienced it at some point in life, when we've gone for something that required taking that extra stroke even though fear told us it could be into oblivion. Don't hesitate.

CHAPTER 6: ACTION

TURNING POINT

Thousands of steps must be taken to bring you to the next one that will be a Turning Point. Yet as simple as it may sound, that one more step must still be taken. Just looking at it will not create the turning point.

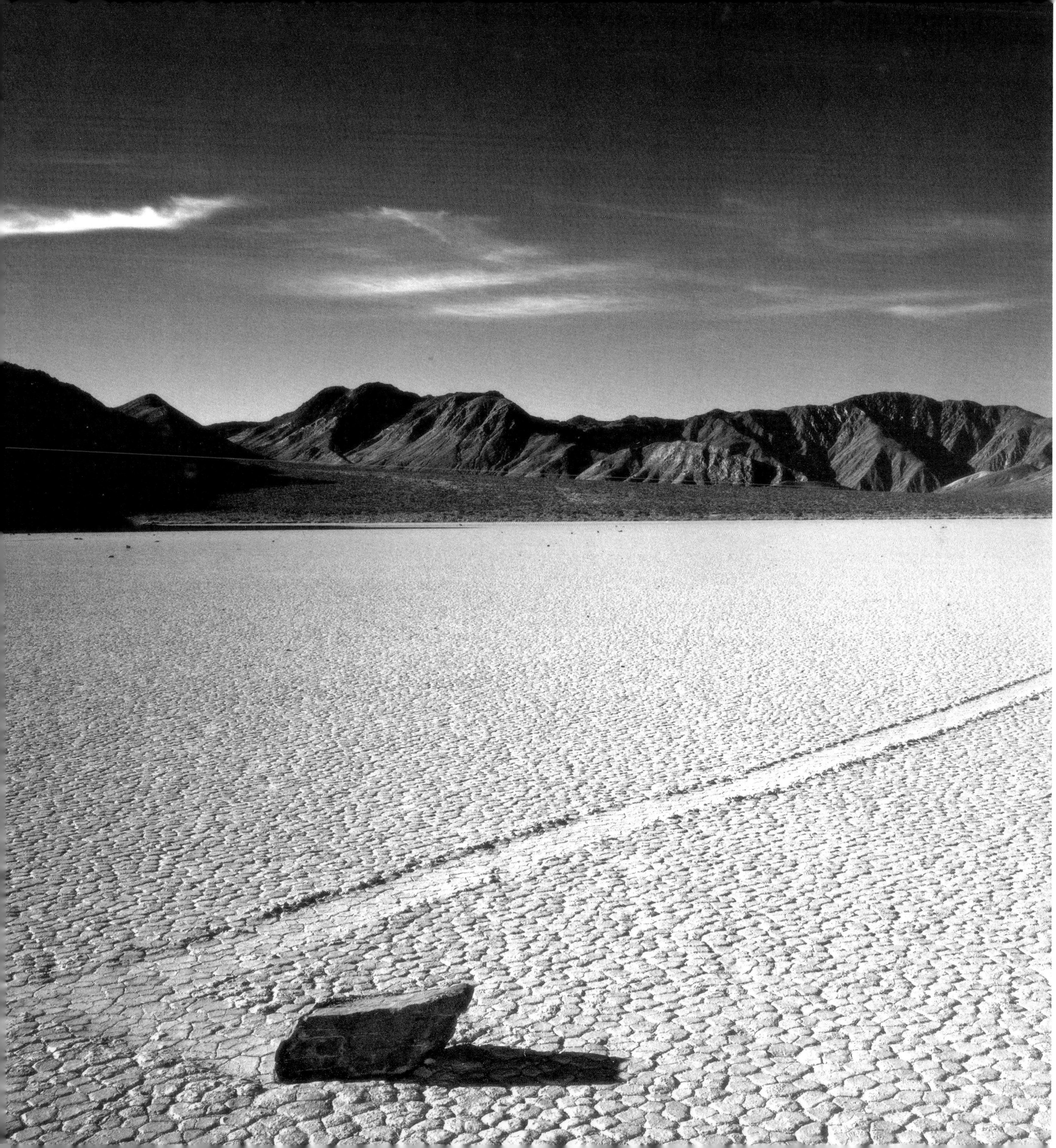

THE ART OF COMPETITION

94

DECISION

A clear Decision is one that can change the course of your life forever.
An unclear decision will only require you to make another that is true later.

ENTHUSIASM

Enthusiasm is the kind of thought or dream that ignites your soul and awakens every cell in your body, filling you with the energy to do something great in your life.

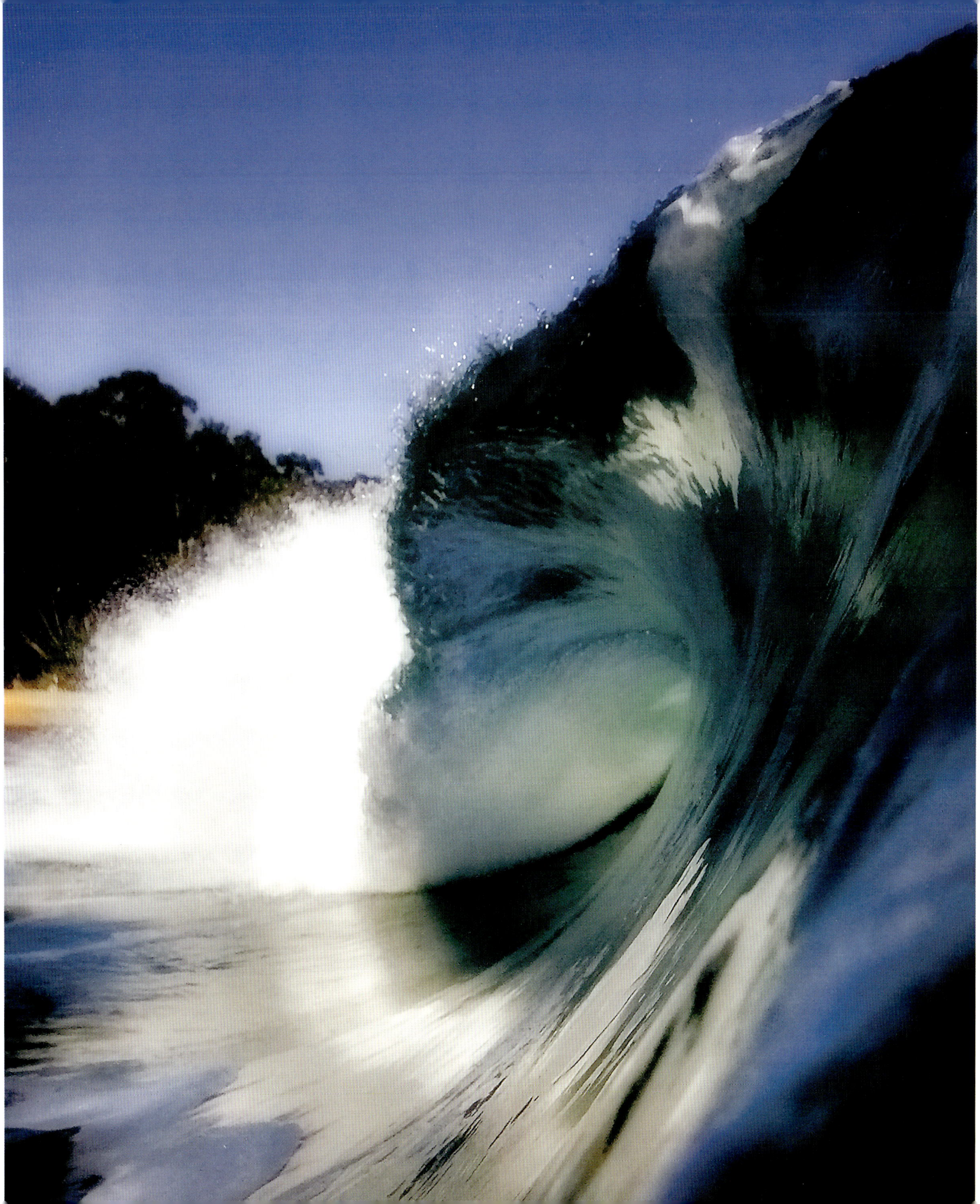

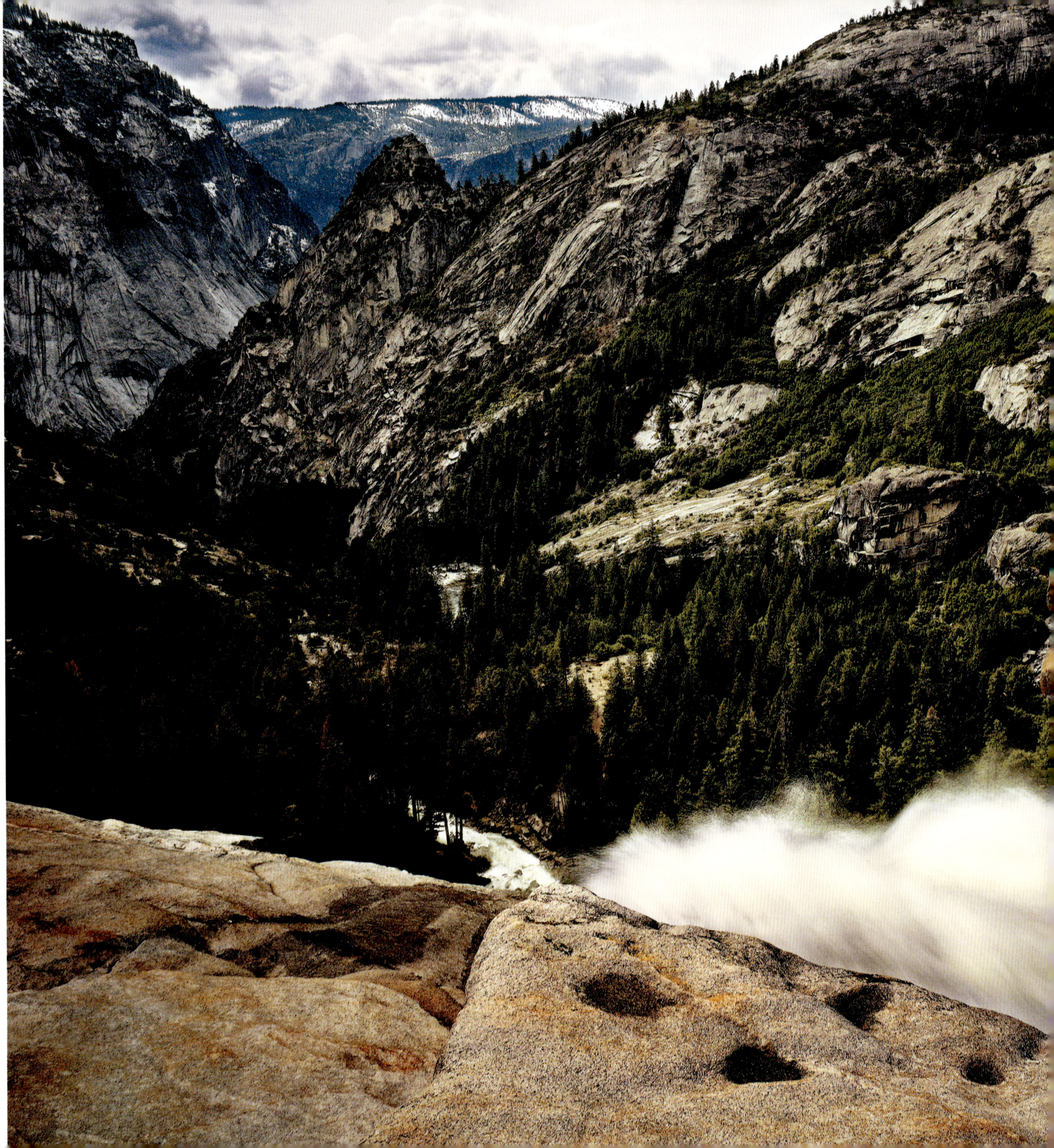

OVERCOMING

Overcoming is best achieved when you become a partner with the reality of a situation and work in cooperation with it rather than fighting it or trying to overpower it. Results with great meaning demand this.

SELF-CONFIDENCE

Self-Confidence is housed in silence. It has no voice or thought, only readiness to take the right action.

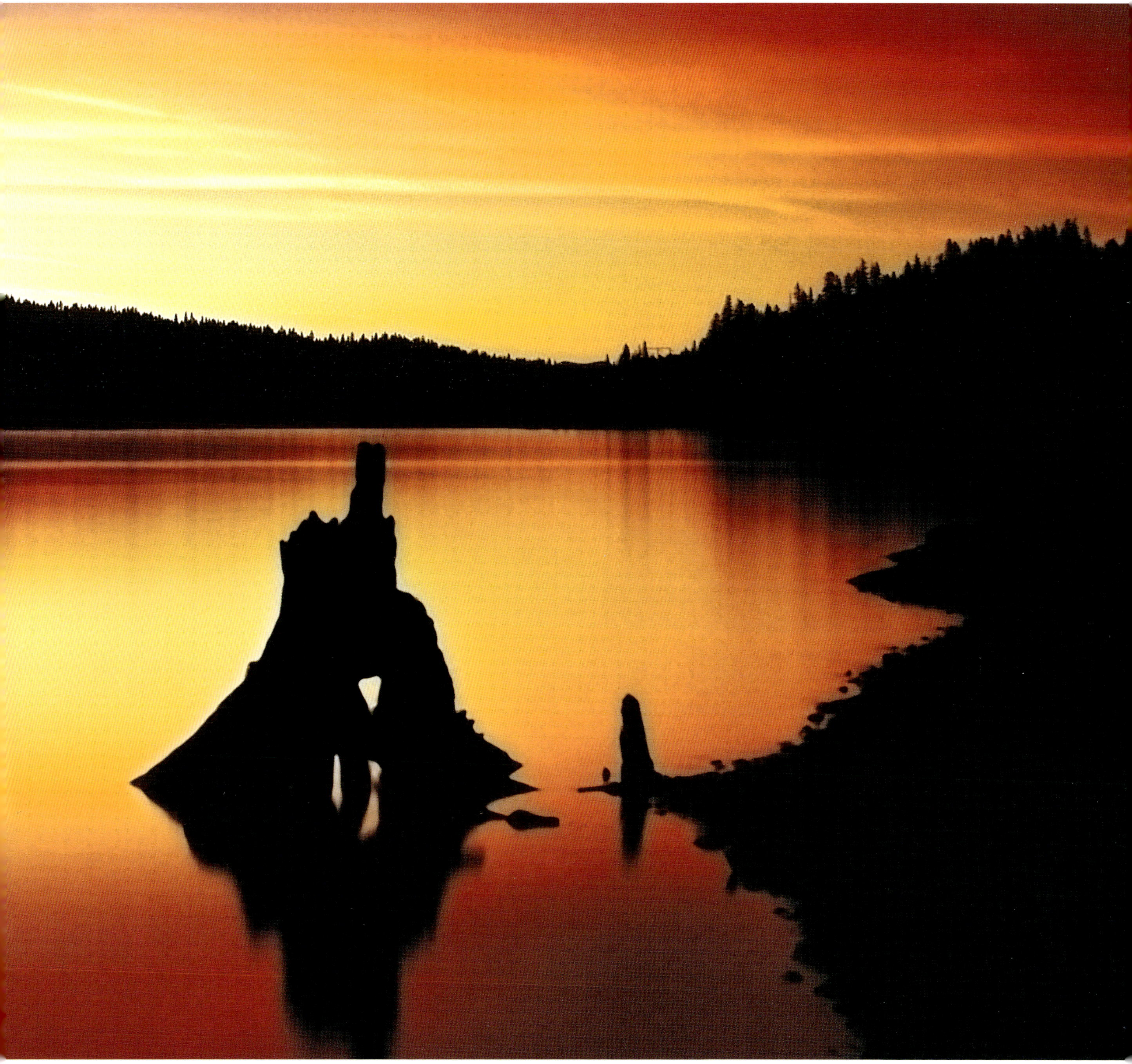

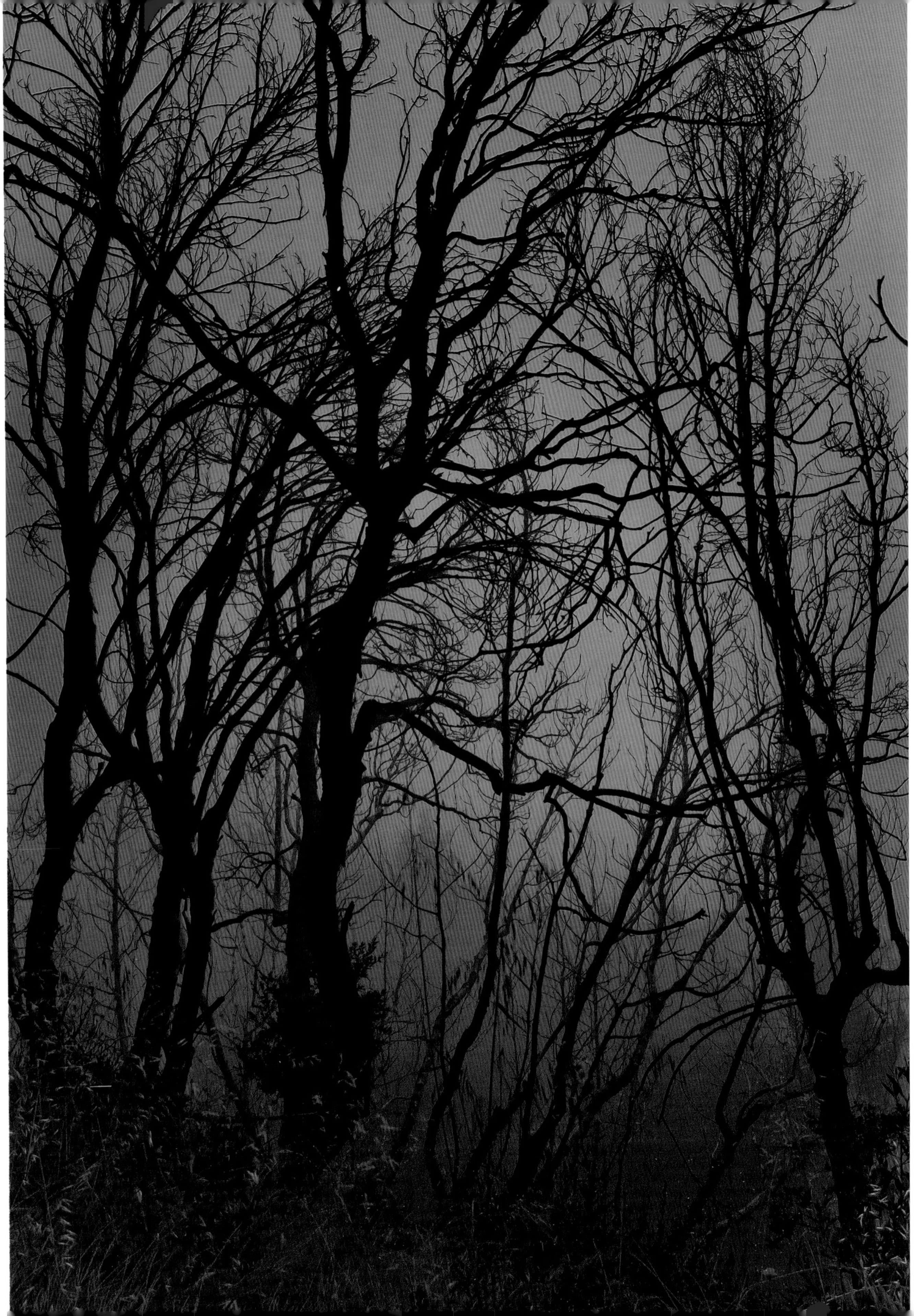

PASSION

Passion is something you will get up early for or stay up late doing without ever knowing it is early or late.

THE ART OF COMPETITION

104

TEMPTATION

Temptation is a teacher of focus and will. Each time our journey starts to falter and we catch ourselves before temptation takes over, we strengthen our ability to hold true to what is really important to us.

REST

Rest is honoring your body and its need to repair physically. It is also essential for recharging your emotional and spiritual batteries. It is the partner to work. When joined together these two powerful forces create magnificence in life.

THE ART OF COMPETITION

BOUNDARY

A Boundary is looking at the impossible. The impossible is simply a solution that has yet to present itself.

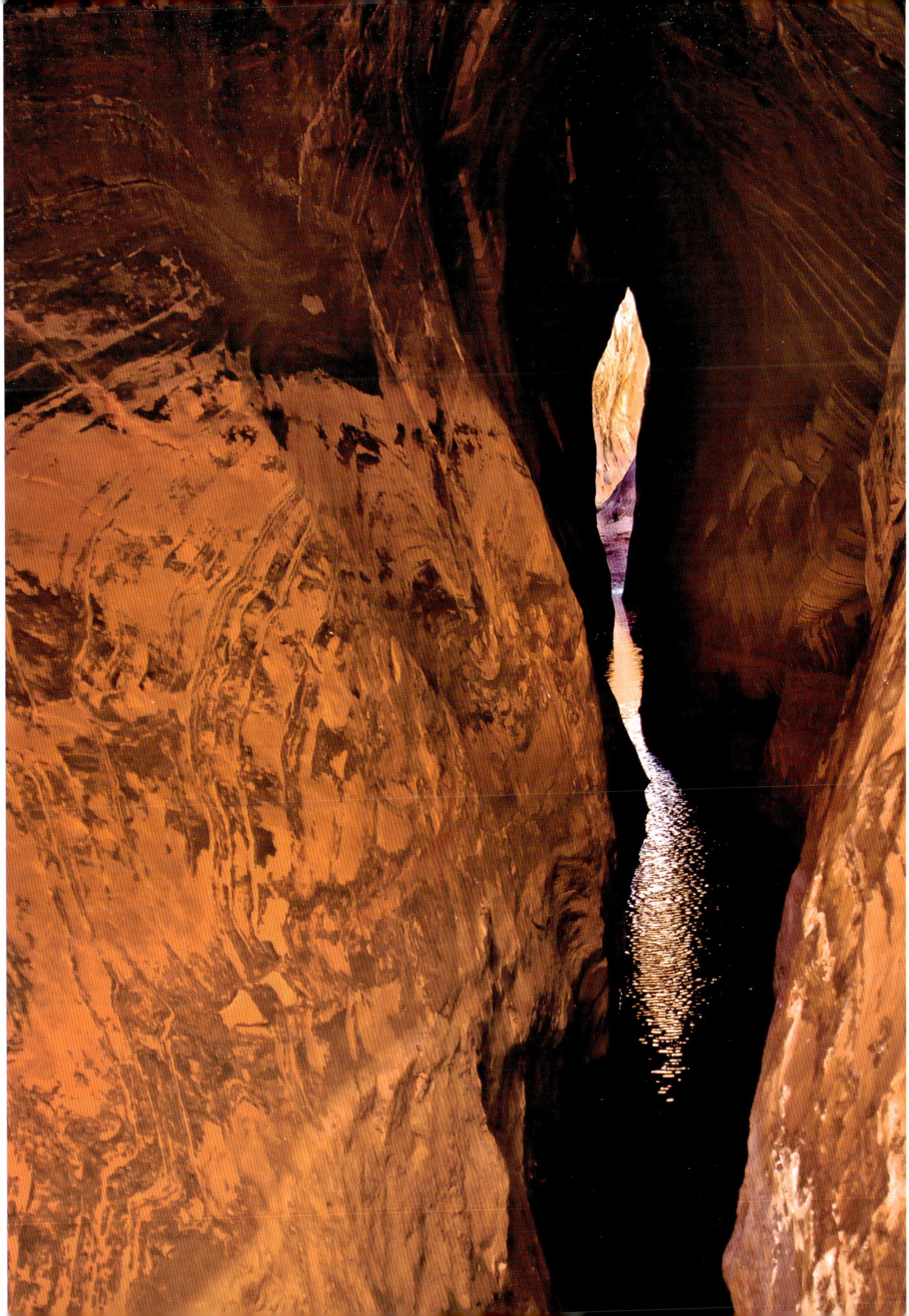

THE ART OF COMPETITION

110

TIME

When you are thinking, Time is linear and you are bound by its measure. When you stop thinking, time is boundless and it accommodates the space necessary for you to experience your potential.

THE ART OF COMPETITION

112

OBSESSIVENESS

Obsessiveness begins one step past the border where commitment ends. It is excessive action that weakens you rather than strengthens you.

DRIVING FORCE

A Driving Force is an overwhelmingly strong part of your being that can either create or destroy your life. If it is positive, learning to harness it will propel you to the greatest of heights. If it is negative it must be diffused until it no longer has weight over you.

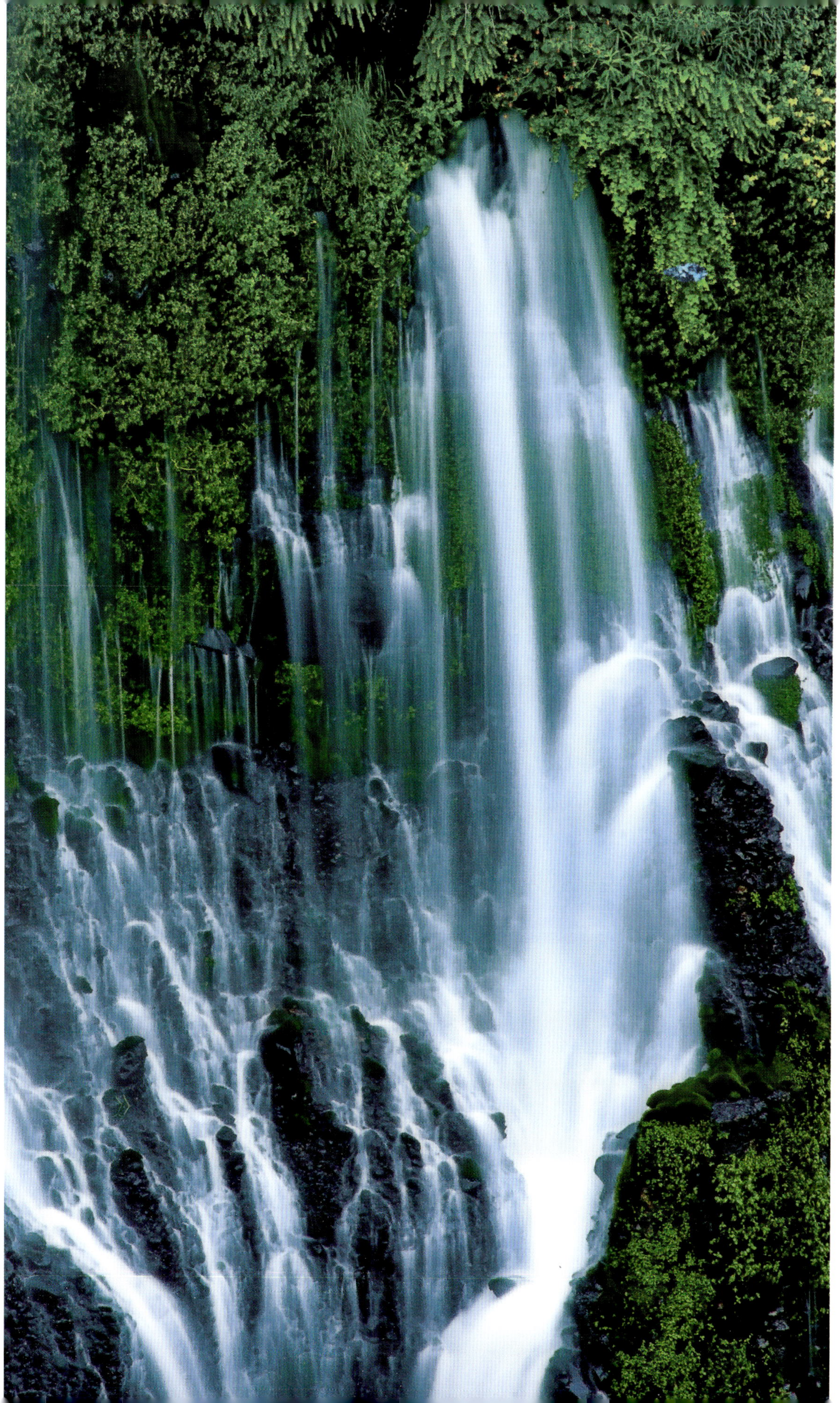

FREEDOM

Real Freedom is living with true purpose, a process that calls for completely engaging in what at times can seem an impossible task. It is rarely achieved without surrendering your humanness to this greater quest.

THE ART OF COMPETITION

THE ART OF COMPETITION

118

ADVENTURE

Adventure is in all things you do that require no coaxing to engage in. They are the journeys you can barely wait to start, yet they are also the ones you are never fully sure of their outcome. Uncertainty is the signature of an adventure.

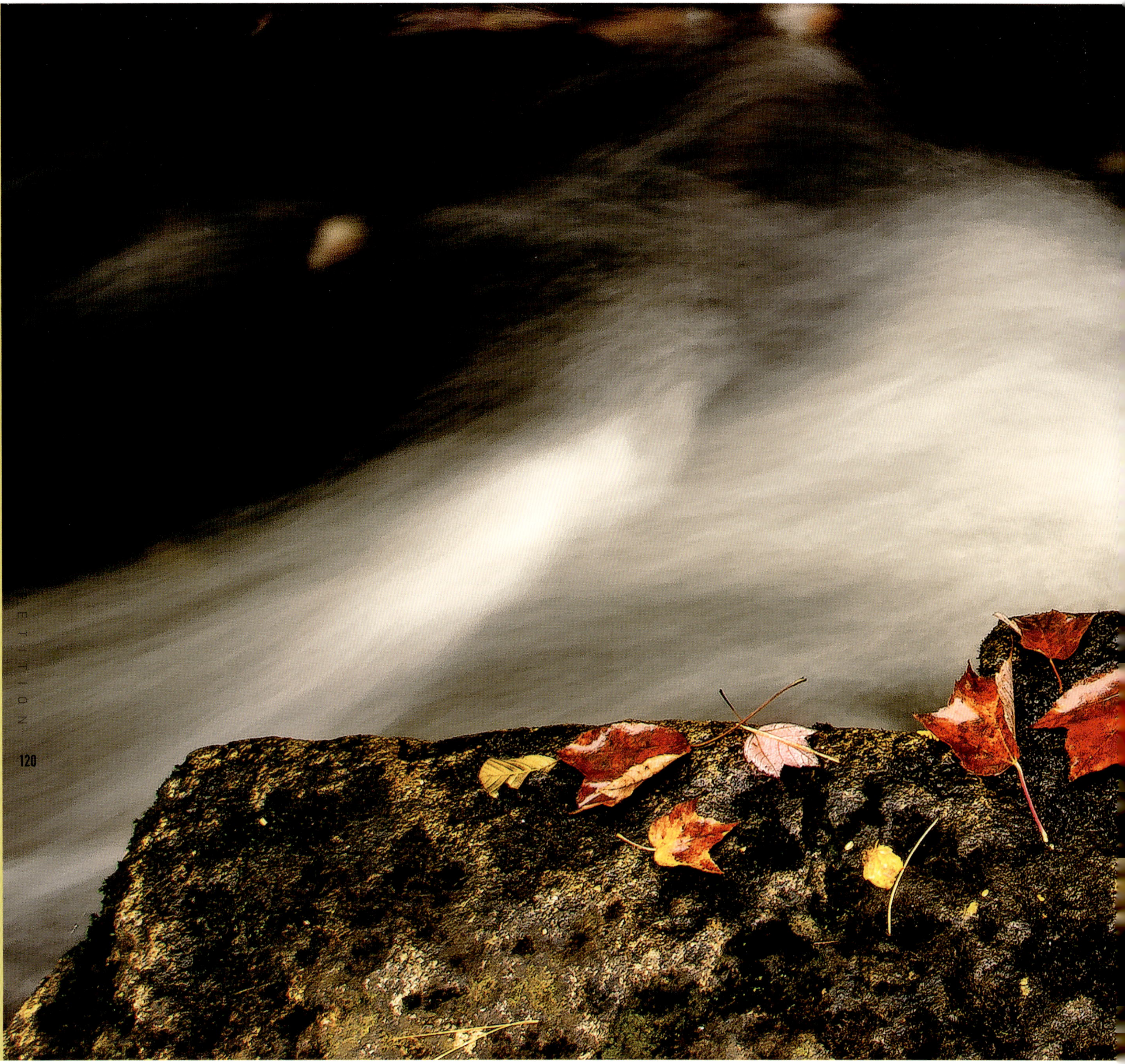

HEALING

Healing is that which makes you a better person. Rarely is it easy, and even less likely is it comfortable. But it is always worth pursuing.

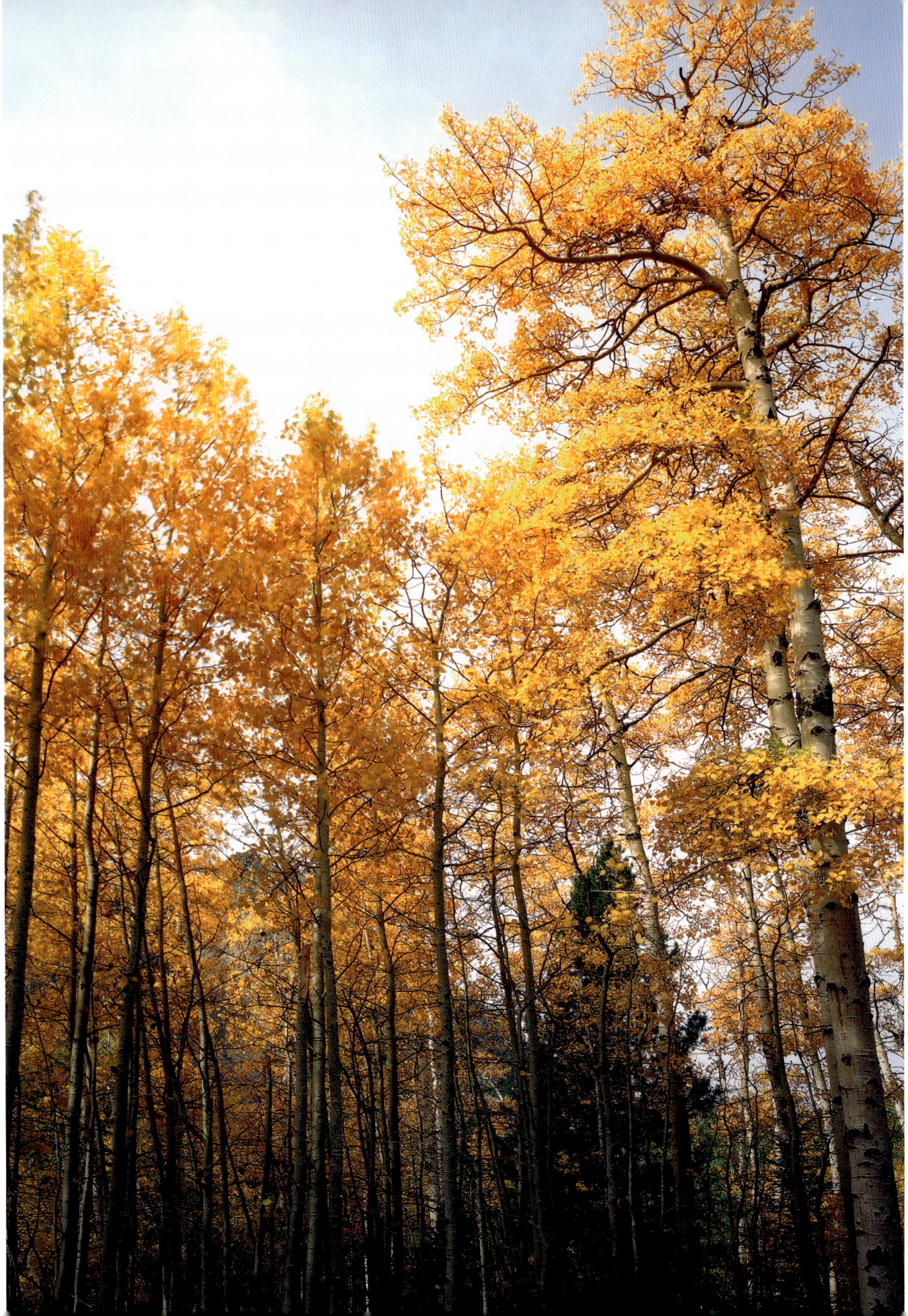

PEAK

Peak is one very short, very small moment of time where the energy generated through countless hours of inglorious preparation are gathered and focused into one heightened expression of personal perfection.

DESIRE

Desire puts your foot on the accelerator. Passion applies the pressure. Clarity steers you in the right direction. Awareness makes sure you don't run out of gas before you arrive.

THE ART OF COMPETITION

THE ART OF COMPETITION

126

SKILL

True Skill is learned through the gradual, diligent practice of a particular technique. Skill reaches mastery when you are capable of employing it fully without any thought of how to do it or concern of its outcome.

THE ART OF COMPETITION

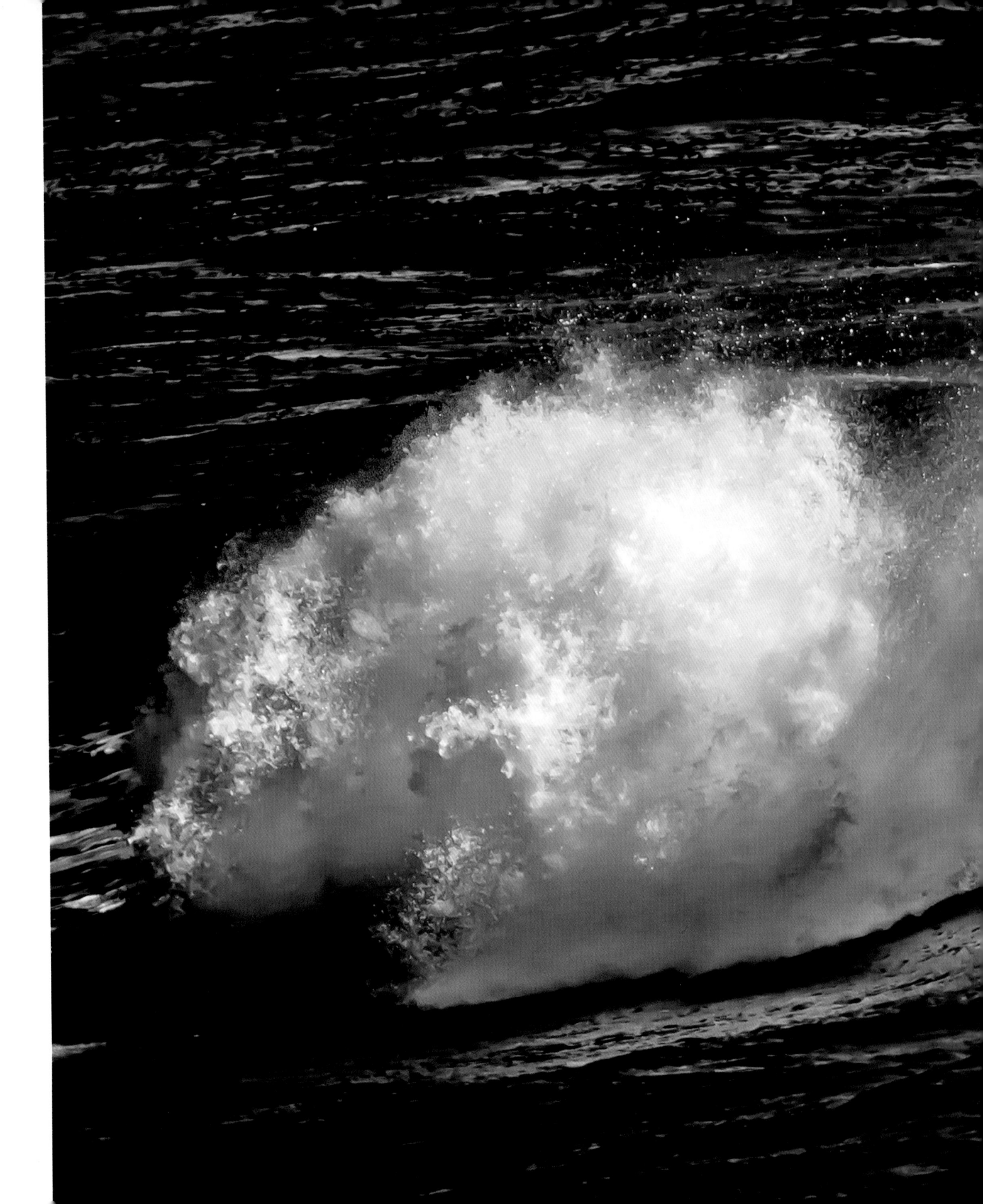

POTENTIAL

Potential is a blank page. You must at some point either pick up the brush and paint or close the book and walk away.

CHAPTER 7: STUCK

The Art of Competition is devoted to flow, to calling up silence to snuff out every ounce of doubt that might hold you back, to allowing every action and thought to break open ordinary limits and take you toward flawlessness. It's taking everything you have perfected through practice, done a thousand times over, then doing it once more, passing it all through the lens of mastery and enjoying the whole effort for its unique and enduring beauty. It will have your fingerprint, embossed and brilliant, as its name. It's a gold medal or a world record. It's a solo run touched by a grace that no one but you will ever see. It's the seductive desire to quit that finally bows down, allowing resiliency to reign supreme.

These are the moments we all strive for. But sometimes it feels more like floundering than flying, where your individual, exquisite capabilities feel locked away, deep and inaccessible. Everyone knows what this barren feeling is like. It can be the times when ideas are just not coming even though deadlines are looming. The longer you sit staring at a blank computer screen hoping for the fresh concept to emerge and save the day, the more emptiness strangles your mind. It's the piles upon untouched piles of life's incomplete commitments that squeeze the life force out of you with their invisible oppressive weight, making it nearly impossible to come up with a positive thought or action that will clean the slate. It's paralyzing. Day after steadfast day you train, trying to perfect your skill with unwavering commitment, but the lack of progress makes your efforts feel like you are just carving a gigantic groove deeper and deeper, one whose direction only seems to lead you farther from your appointment with destiny. You feel stuck. What can you do? Strong-arm the universe into conforming to your wishes? Not likely! Give up because you have had enough of spinning your wheels with no apparent forward progress? That critical moment of relief when the pendulum starts swinging back in your favor rarely happens as quickly as is hoped! Do you keep banging away so that at least you can say you tried, even though you have nothing to show for your efforts? Busy and effective are rarely on the same page!

There is hope when we are stuck! Tap into the Art of Competition. Tap into the mindset of a champion, of you as a champion. Allow patience to rule supreme. Endless hours go into unleashing the flow that one would call Art. Until then "stuck" can simply be amalgamating the requisite amount of personal force necessary to gain traction and move closer to your goals. It may take a thousand pounds of accumulated effort to dissolve the barrier that keeps you stuck in this exact instant. Don't quit at nine hundred and ninety-nine pounds. Go until you have a thousand and one. Then watch the ease with which your efforts bond with your dreams to create something significant, something your soul would have missed out on had you not taken that final, breakthrough step.

Challenge is mostly visible when you stand and look in its mirror. Wind blowing against a cyclist is only a challenge if the rider is present. Without the rider, it is simply beautiful wind blowing. You are in the middle, between the reflection of challenge and the brilliant light of excellence. But as we all know, pressing forward can wear on your reserves and your desire, especially when "stuck" has "progress" in a choke hold. In those precarious moments of dwindling hope, tap into the power that drawing back to regroup can bring. This is not giving up! Regrouping is a champion's way of gathering new force while letting the challenge expend itself until it has little left to offer, then engaging again with enough might to scatter whatever small stones still remain in the way of your greatness.

Regrouping is the universal space necessary for reflection to move past being stuck, even if it takes place in the smallest fraction of a second. Is changing course the imperative? If so, collect your belongings and engage with the new path that is true.

Is your current course still the calling? Often it is, even if it's a supreme effort to turn and look ahead once more. Draw inward long enough to see the challenge from a slightly different angle. Now relaunch fully with new hope, new insight and new force, the force of a champion, the force that is the Art of Competition.

CHAPTER 8: ENGAGE

FEARING UNCERTAINTY IS PARALYZING.
EMBRACING IT IS GALVANIZING.

THE ART OF COMPETITION

135

THE ART OF COMPETITION

A RACE IS TRUTH IN MOTION.

THE ART OF COMPETITION

137

ONE IS NOT OWED VICTORY JUST BECAUSE OF HARD TRAINING;
IT MUST STILL BE EARNED ON THE DAY OF COMPETITION.

THE ART OF COMPETITION

INNER PEACE, THEN OUTER RESULTS;
NOT THE OTHER WAY AROUND.

141

THE ART OF COMPETITION

THE ART OF COMPETITION

| THERE IS NO SACRIFICE IN PURSUITS OF THE HEART.

142

THE ART OF COMPETITION

143

THE ART OF COMPETITION

144

USE PRESSURE TO FOCUS ENERGY.

THE ART OF COMPETITION

145

PERFECTION HAS ITS OWN SILENCE,
FILLED WITH ALL THAT YOU NEED.

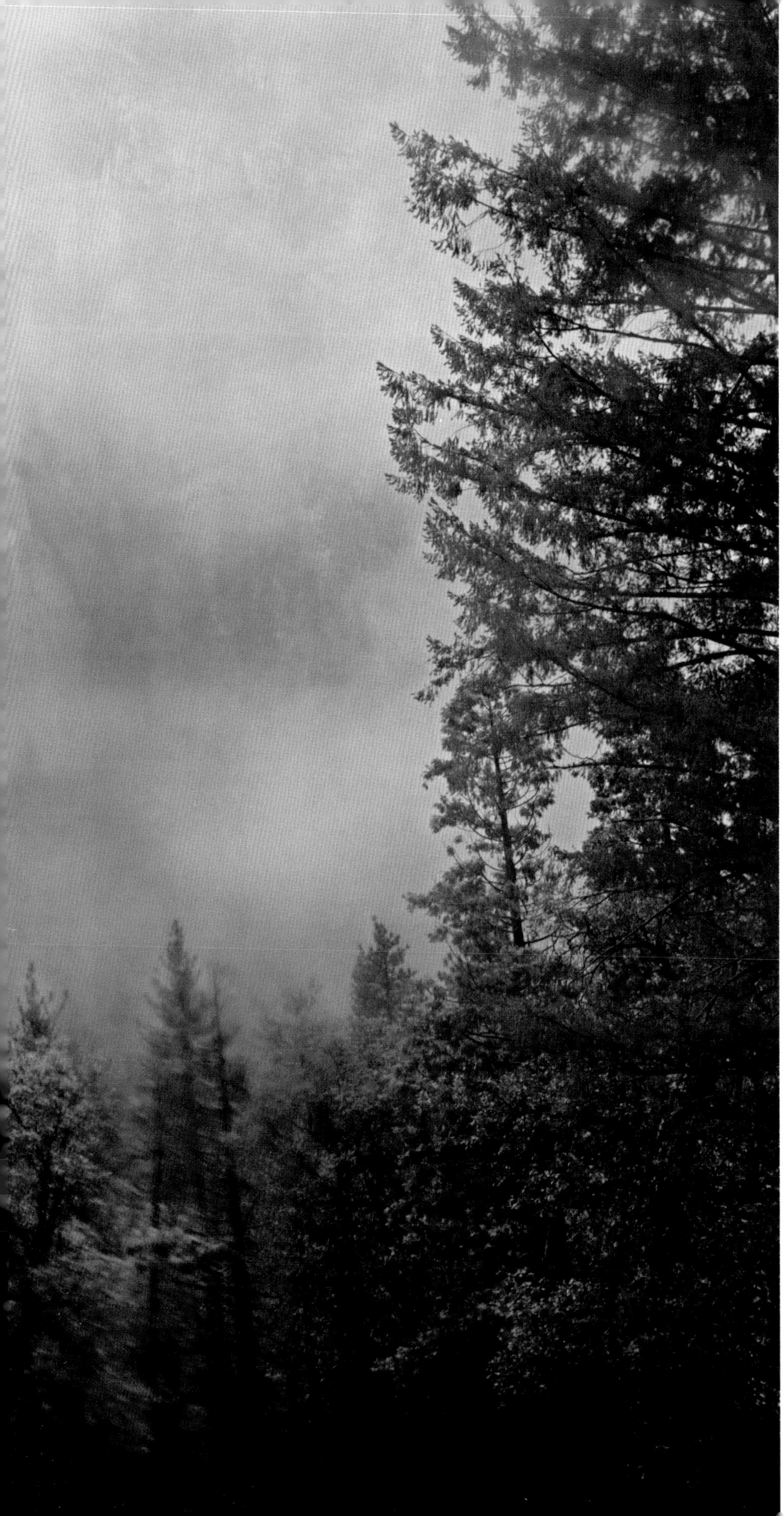

PAIN IS THE SONG OF THE WORKING BODY.
INTENSE PAIN IS ITS SYMPHONY.
ENJOY THE MUSIC.

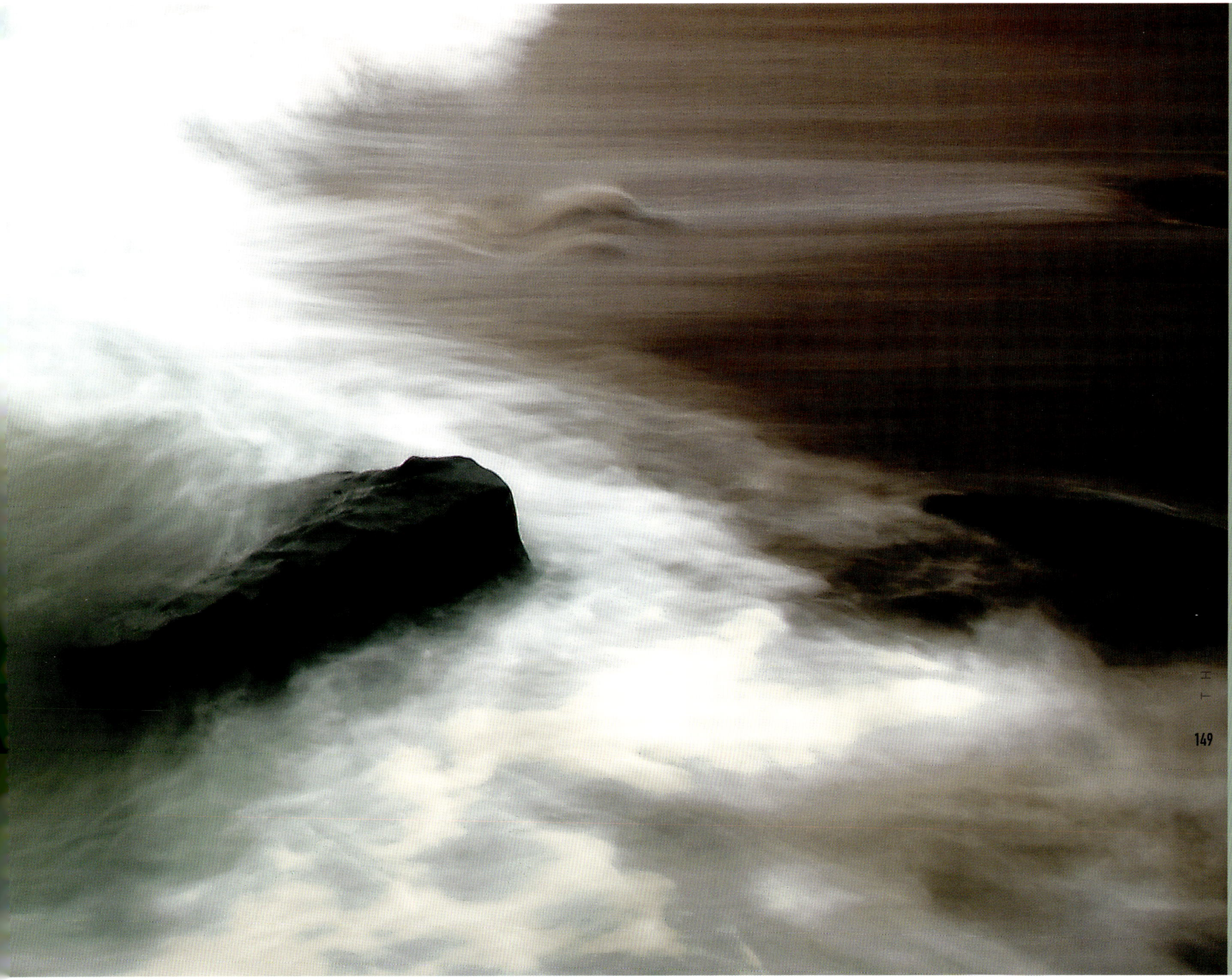

THE ART OF COMPETITION

YOU ARE HALF WAY THERE WHEN
THE JOURNEY IS NINETY PERCENT COMPLETE.

THE ART OF COMPETITION

THE ART OF COMPETITION

152

DESIRE GETS YOU WITHIN SIGHT OF GREATNESS.
SURRENDER ENABLES YOU TO EMBRACE IT.

THE GREATEST VICTORIES CAN'T BE SEEN.

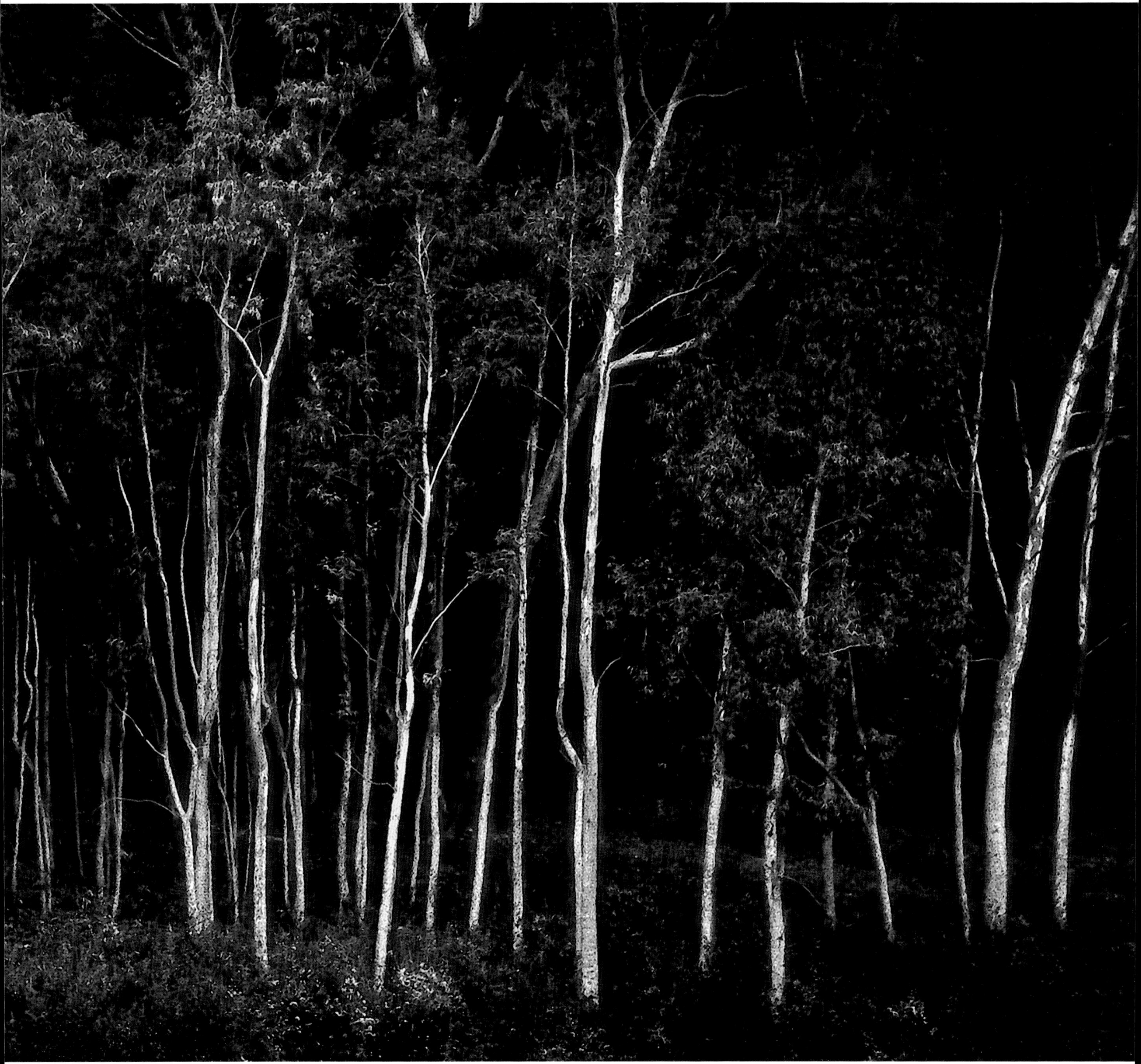

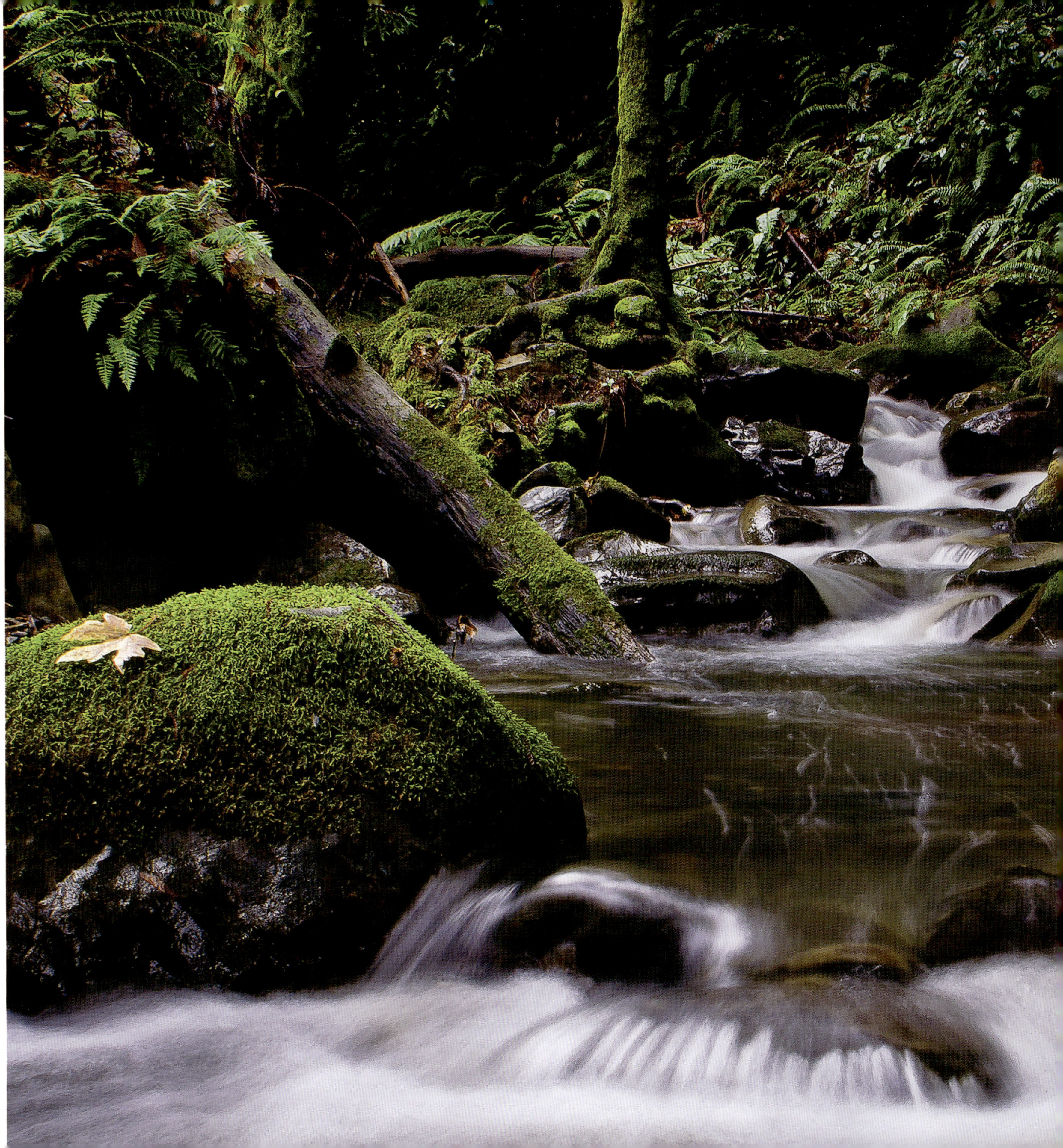

THOUGHT PRECEDES FORM;
SILENCE PRECEDES PERFECT FORM.

THERE IS NEVER A PERFECT RACE,
                  BUT YOU CAN RACE PERFECTLY.

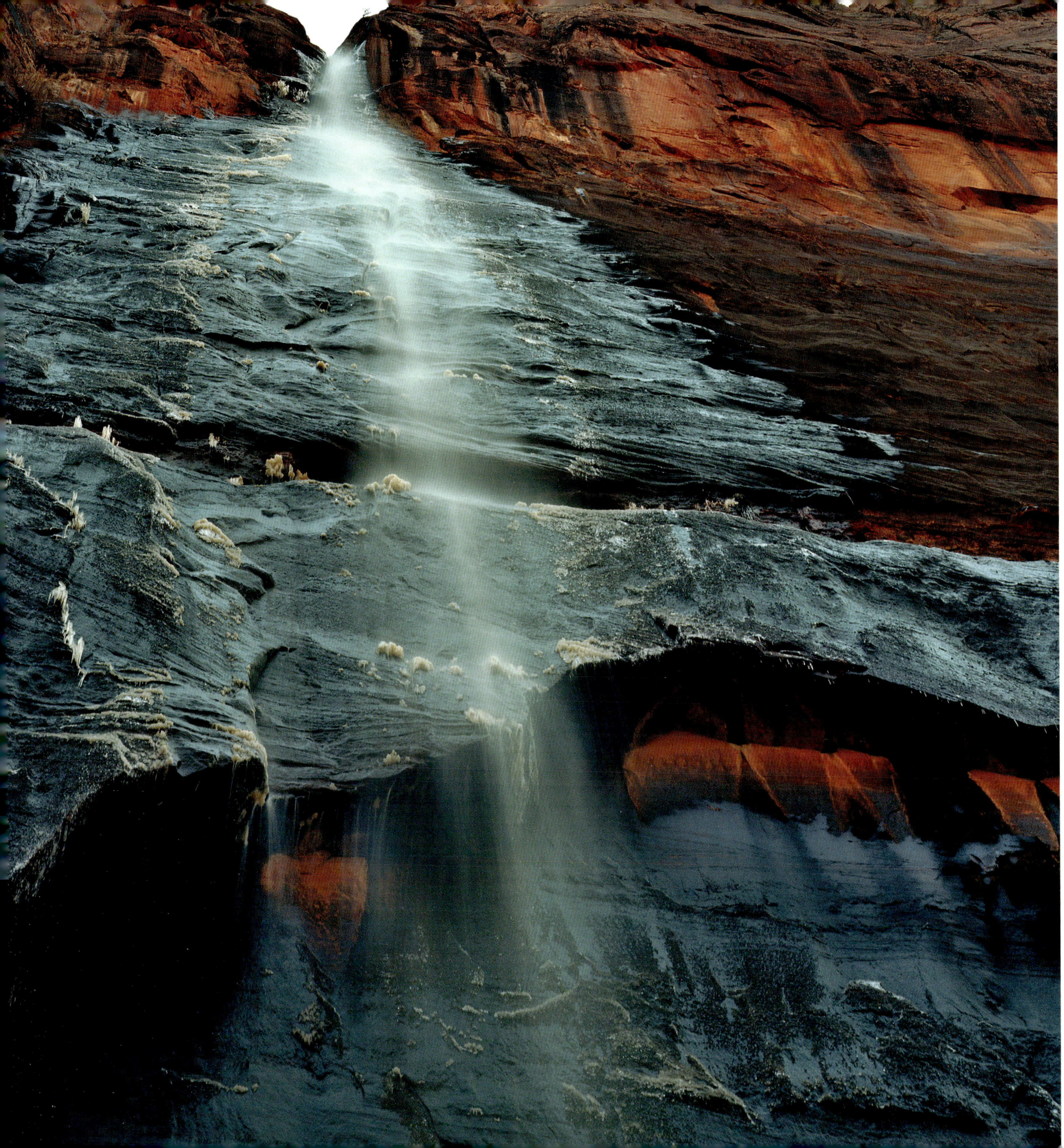

IMPOSSIBLE IS A GREAT VICTORY TAKING SHAPE.

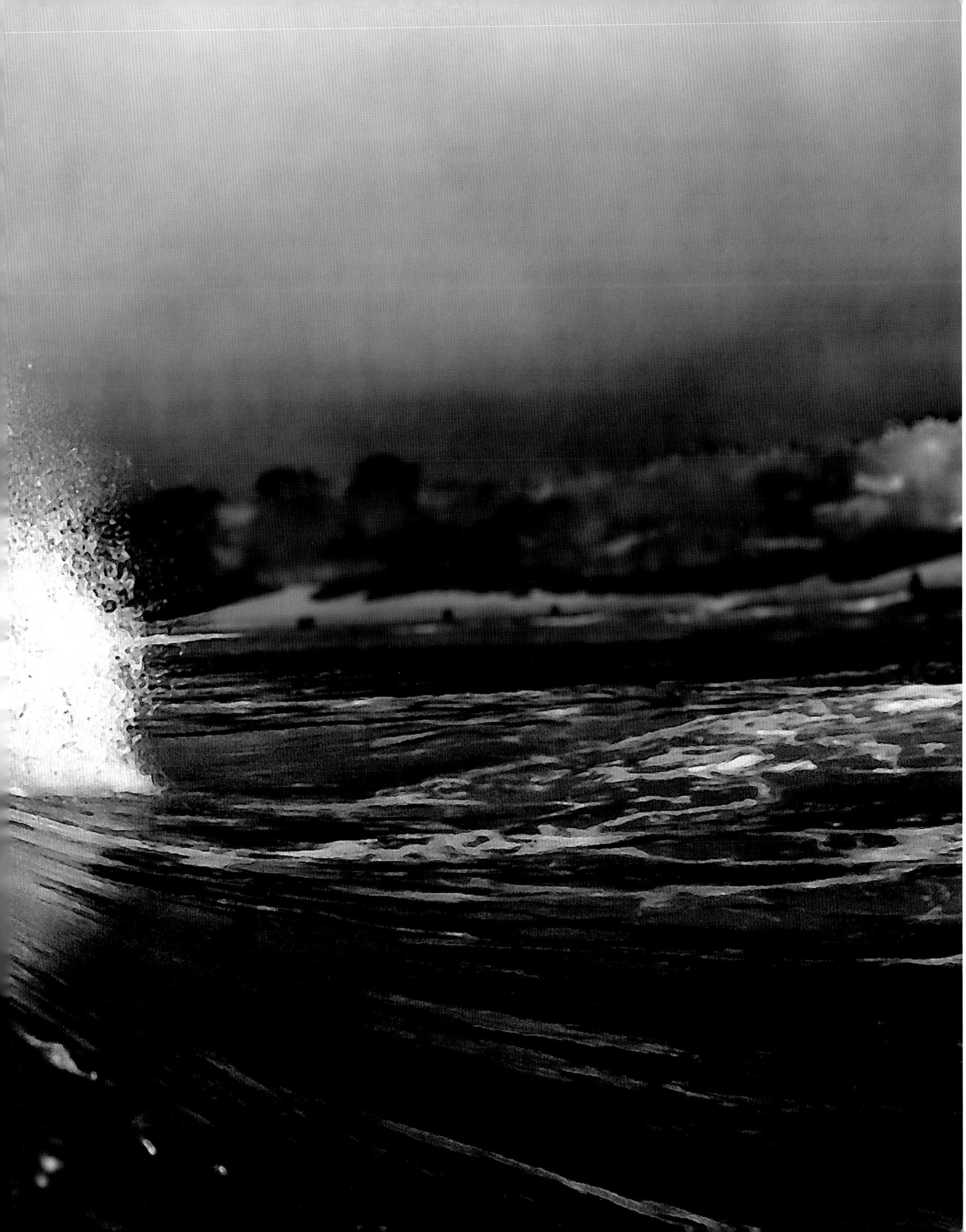

MILLIONS OF REASONS WILL BEG YOU TO QUIT.
WAIT AND LISTEN FOR THE ONE GOOD ONE
THAT REQUIRES YOU TO CONTINUE.

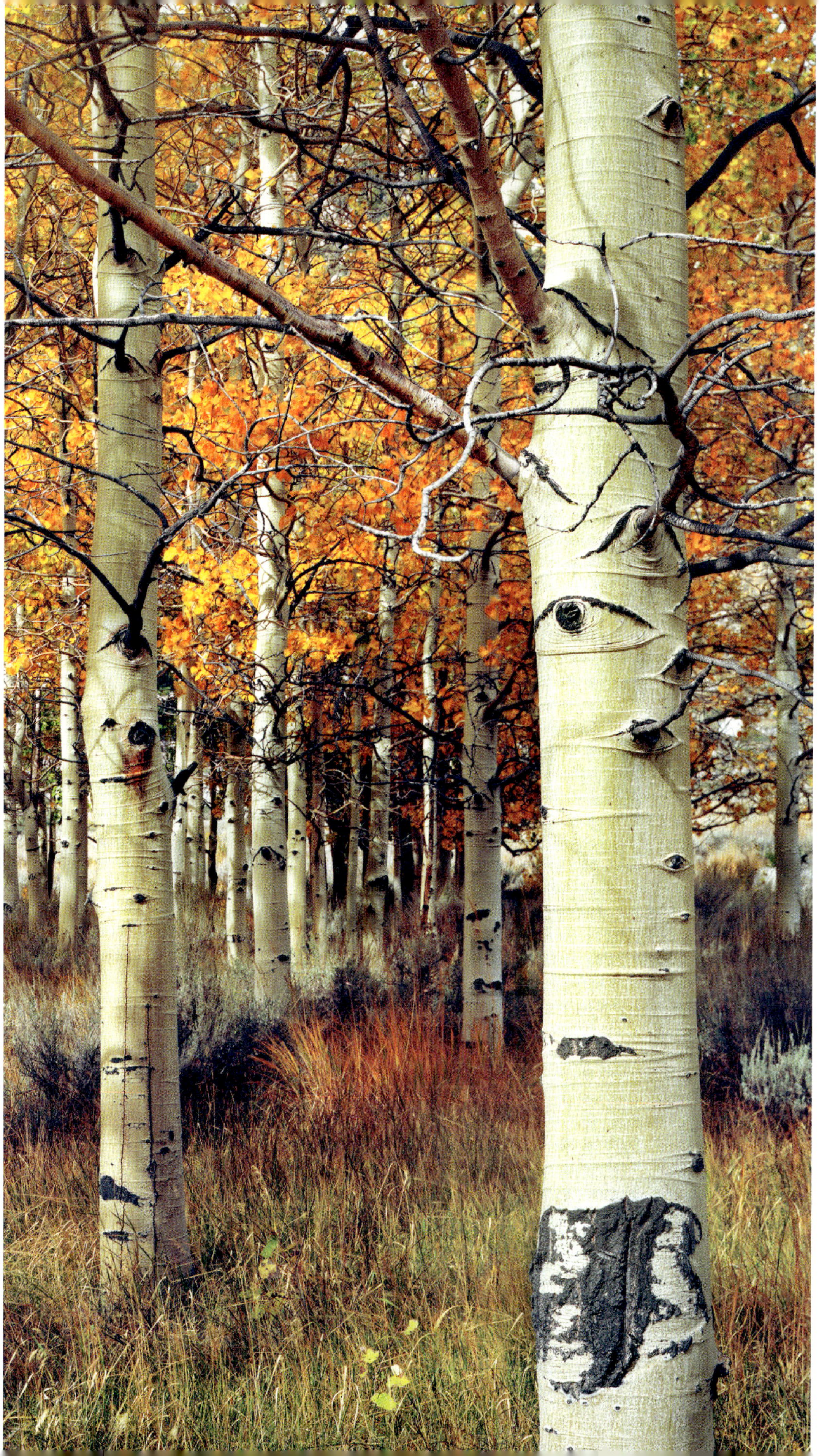

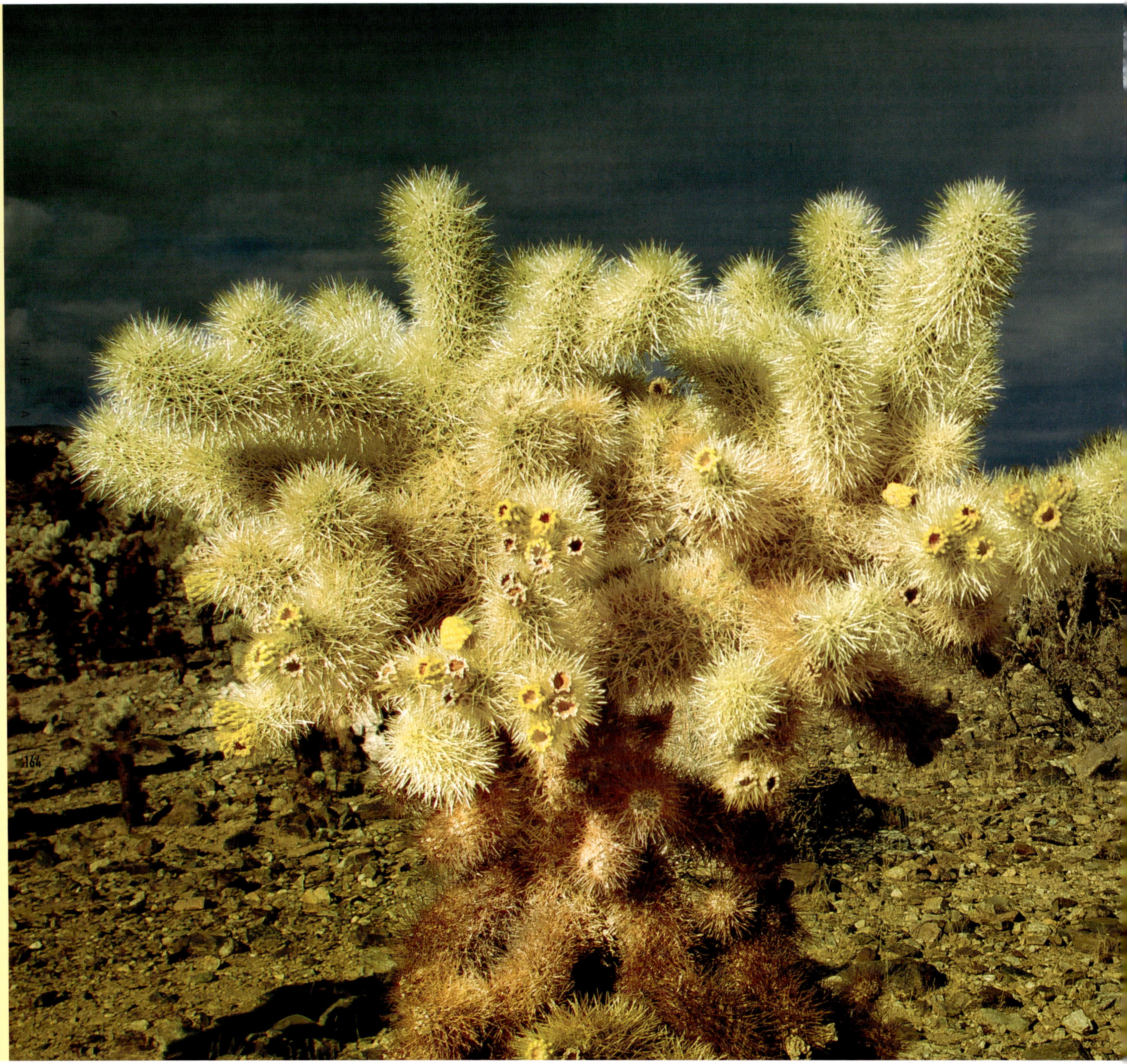

NO TWO BATTLES ARE THE SAME.

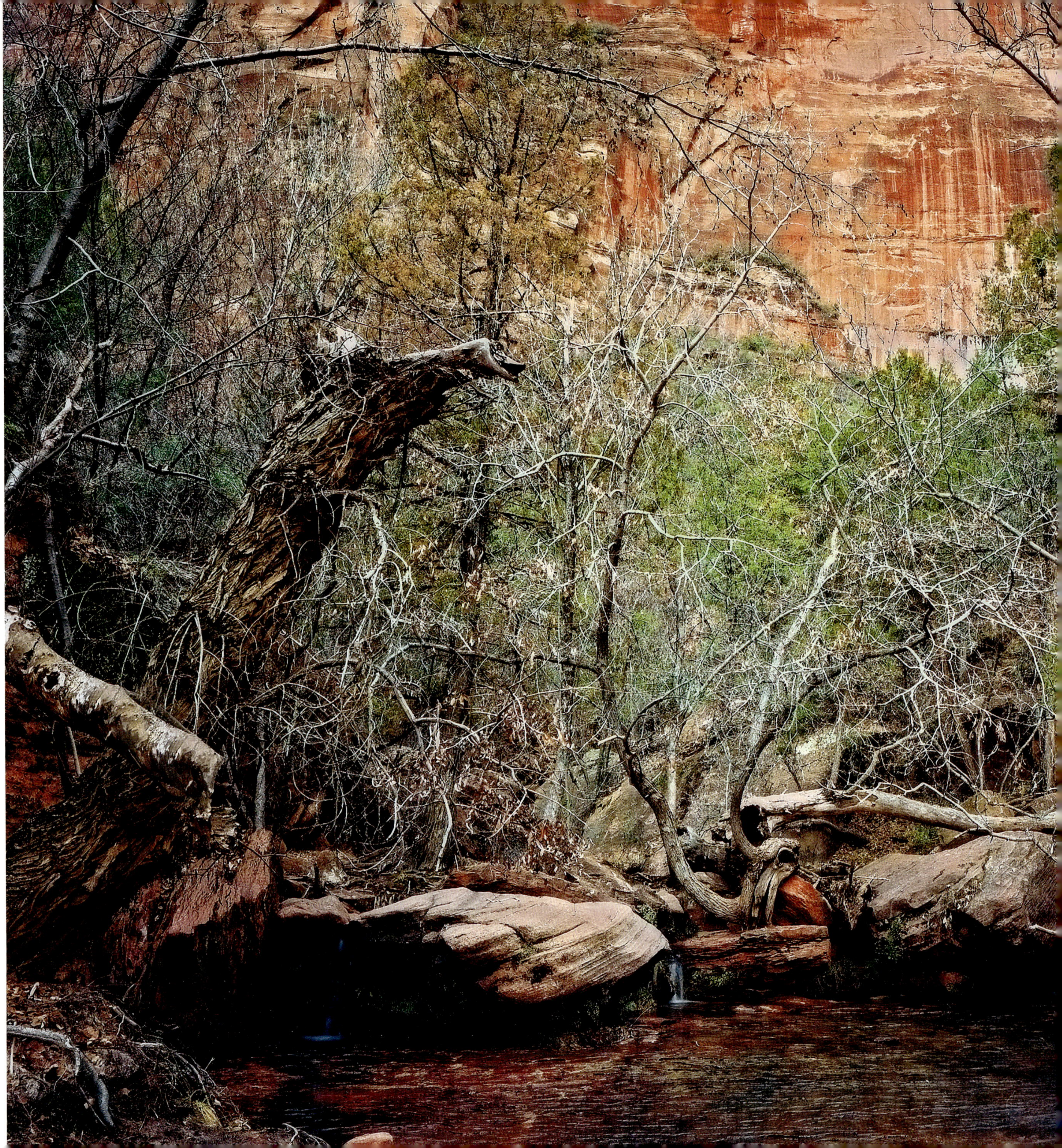

EXPECT CHAOS
AND RESPOND APPROPRIATELY.

THE ART OF COMPETITION

THE ART OF COMPETITION

168

| EVEN CHAMPIONS STRUGGLE.

THE ART OF COMPETITION

169

KONA, HAWAII, OCTOBER 14, 1989.

I was engaged in one of the greatest duels in triathlon history, fighting one of the toughest competitors this sport has ever spawned. We had been in sight of each other for nearly eight hours of relentless head-to-head racing. Our battle began long before the day's starting cannon signaled the official commencement of what many call the toughest single day in sports. Our history together is long and has chapters written at triathlons all over the world. But this one race would become the bar all others would be measured against. Before this singularly defining day, Ironman was considered a survival contest. After its close there would be no other option than to race it.

I was battling six-time Hawaii Ironman Champion Dave Scott, a brilliant athlete who broke every imaginable level of excellence the triathlon world had known.

CHAPTER 9: ART

I had a certain amount of credibility as a viable challenger going into that year's competition, but not nearly enough to make Dave weak-kneed with fear. In fact, he seemed to be racing me more like I was an annoying tick than a true threat to his reign.

For eight solid hours we raced within whispering distance of each other. Swim done. Bike completed. The marathon to close it out became a footrace of four sweat-soaked, blistered feet calling out the pain of the day with each moment of contact on a searing hot roadway. No more than a few inches separated our bodies, but our minds were worlds apart. He was tracking things like caloric intake, undulations in the road and likely terrain changes where he would try to break me. I was quickly melting under the nonstop world-record pace he was pushing us both to sustain.

I didn't know what it took to win the Ironman. I had raced it six times previously, finishing in the top five in all but one. But second is not first. And now, to match Dave's pace, I was going faster than any human on the planet had previously covered 140.6 total miles of swimming, cycling and running. It was drawing down my reserves at a rate that I knew would empty my tank well before the finish line.

A dream can get veiled by reality, and then become so hidden that your grip on that dream loosens to the point where it's just gone. Then the only things left echoing loud and relentlessly are the destructive words our lesser selves use to talk us into giving up, into quitting. And if we listen it will all sound so justified.

I'd just crossed that threshold. My grasp on hope had slackened just enough to open the trapdoor that leads to all places negative. There were close to thirteen miles left in the marathon. Dave was absolutely determined to win: he was dictating the pace of the race. I had no other choice but to try to glue myself to his side. An inch lost was a race lost.

He began surging at a devastatingly fast pace that I could no longer match. Fortunately, there is a slight delay between when your mind gives up, and your body, that temple you have trained countless hours so that you can push through these moments of doubt, will actually follow the marching orders and begin to slow. It's kind of like holding your breath. It takes a while before the lack of oxygen does its damage. Somewhere between the last breath drawn that still brought hope and the current one soaked with toxic thoughts, a different reality took hold and helped me out.

In the days leading up to the race, I had seen a photo of a great Huichol Indian shaman in a magazine. His name was Don José Matsuwa. He lived in Mexico: he was 110 years old. His face had a life's worth of stories written on it, but the one that shined the brightest was the one saying he was happy just to be alive. I knew that feeling. It was recognizable. It's how I feel when I am lost in the beauty of the Colorado Rockies during a long trail run. Or the bond I make with life when the winter storms kick up monstrous frothing waves, and I feel their powerful breath as they break all the way out to the horizon and beyond.

In that momentary delay between hope and despair, between giving it my all and giving it all up, my mind fell silent. That's a huge transition to make— to go from pursuing your dream with every ounce of passion you have to allowing yourself to embrace the possibility that maybe, just maybe, you don't have what it takes to fulfill that purpose, to admit you will never ever make your greatest dream a reality.

The world fell silent. I was waiting for the inevitable to overpower me, to hear the one lethal thought that gags all hope and crushes possibility: "I Can't Do It." But it never got a chance, because in that one precious moment of silence, Don José's image came back to me. He was there, happy just to be alive!

And suddenly, I was happy just to be there in the race, the greatest race our sport had ever seen, one where—if I could hold on— I would better my previous finishing time by a whopping thirty minutes! And I was holding on, running stride for stride with the best guy in the world, still giving him a run for his money. He didn't know I was a scant hair's width away from giving it all up. Maybe I could fool him a bit longer and just maybe this moment of utter despair would be temporary. Maybe my energy would return along with my will, my dream and the best I could offer on that day.

We continued, side by side, until the last long uphill that separates never-ending miles of racing through barren lava from the sight of an endless sea of cheering faces at the finish line. That now famous rise was where I had the ounce extra I needed to make a move, and Dave was left scouring the walls of a completely empty vat for scraps to help him hold on. He found none.

I won my first Ironman World Championship that day by a mere fifty-eight seconds in a battle that many called the greatest race our sport has ever seen. But the greatest race of my career would not come until six years later when I would be vying for my sixth and final Ironman World Championship title.

BOULDER, COLORADO, JULY 1995

A lot had happened in six years. I had a son who was almost two, a being well worth loving and cherishing. His presence had catalyzed significant changes in my training. I'd slimmed down the extras that were mostly testing sessions invented to reinforce my self-confidence. In their place, pared down and basic, were the nitty-gritties that wouldn't fully show their valor until race day. This took unwavering trust. But time as a father trumped the few extra workouts each week that did little for bottom line fitness.

My string of Ironman titles was at five, but deep inside I could feel I was paying the price. My reserves felt uncharacteristically low. There'd only been a paltry week's worth of days total since the beginning of the year that I felt fully charged up and capable of going full force in my training. Compounding that issue was the fact that, well, I was now thirty-seven years old. I was ancient by endurance standards, and every one of my competitors had put a small but significant check into their column of advantages that they would exploit and use against me on race day.

Fortunately, psychology is always a factor in race dynamics. I was still riding the updraft created by my previous victories. World records fell in three of those previous triumphs, and in the eyes of most of my competitors I was as unbeatable as it gets at the Ironman, at my game. They fought, year after year with every tool they could muster, pushing me to the limit. But it was never quite enough to break the ironclad hold I had on the Ironman recipe for success. Some said I had rewritten the book on performance, unlocked its code, that I was its master. I was not as confident in my capabilities as they were.

Motivation is the powerhouse that initiates all great action. It's best when found before the first step toward a goal gets initiated. It helps chart your course and serves as a solid anchor against the most rugged landslides ahead that could derail your efforts. If motivated and fueled with a dream, you are likely to persevere no matter what. Without it, the smallest of hiccups can stall your efforts forever.

I had to find it. I needed good reason to once more put in 15,000 miles of training in less than a year's time. Five titles sounded about as nice as any number out there. Maybe it was time to segue smoothly and seamlessly out of racing and into something less physically demanding. Tick, tock. I could feel it.

The clear and obvious incentive would be to go for number six. Dave Scott amassed that number of Hawaii Ironman titles during his career. I was at five! One more victory would put me in a club that had an elite membership of one solitary warrior. I'd like to be part of that club! But that wasn't enough. Winning is not necessarily meaning or motivation. It's a goal, a dream, but it does not come dripping with significance. It can't automatically elevate your game to art, to guarantee a performance that will be lasting in the minds of others, and more importantly, bring you something that will alter your inner being on a fundamental level. There are a lot of winners in the world. Not all are of them are happy!

I knew that even a dozen victories would just be a dozen victories if nothing was learned from them, and while they would feel great, they might just as well be a dozen defeats if they didn't add depth to my character, teach me about competition, enhance my understanding of the world. Those insights are the real treasure. Prize money gets spent. Articles are soon forgotten, stashed silently away on a shelf, never read again. Television broadcasts and interviews are rarely replayed. What truly lives on are the things you grasp through a great contest that get used in the immediate workings of life, the nuggets that clearly smooth the surface of daily existence that were learned by trial when it was all being put on the line in competition.

I knew I had to go back to the Ironman once more. It wouldn't be with the overwhelming desire of winning. It would be to gain one last piece of myself that only competition could bestow. There was some lesson still calling me that made it imperative to return.

My goal, my motivation, was more personal and less quantifiable than victory. I wanted to bring absolute personal perfection, total engagement and a full embrace to race day no matter how unsightly, unappealing or unpleasant it got. That was not a negative measure of how I felt it would be. It simply explains the expanse of my commitment should the journey unfold differently than my ideal would have it. I would call up my best no matter the gravity being exerted by uncertainty or the amount of distance separating me from my chance at bringing home number six. I didn't have the word for it at the time, but I was committed to turning my final Ironman into athletic art.

Unfortunately, there was a deep, pounding problem that was clenching tighter with every passing day. I was tired. My reserves were severely depleted. Recovery was discouragingly slow. Ironman was approaching but my chance of success was waning. Art and exhaustion rarely hold hands. Things don't have to be ideal to be perfectly executed, but the narrow corridor of solutions to tough challenges is exceedingly difficult to navigate when fatigue lines the walls and the exit point cannot be seen.

One ray of hope would begin to shine the exact week when every other Ironman competitor turned their focus toward the last push of incredibly challenging but necessary workouts in preparation for October's final exam. It would come during an August retreat in the wilds of Alaska. The leader of the workshop was a critically important individual whose connection goes back to that very first moment I saw Don José's image in a magazine. It was Don José's adopted grandson, also a shaman, named Brant Secunda.

I met Brant shortly after that first breakthrough victory in Kona and had been studying with him since. Both he and Don

José were featured in the magazine I'd seen two days before my showdown with Dave Scott. It explained that they would be teaching about the way of life that comes from the Huichol Indians of Mexico. I would later learn of the priceless value the Huichols put on developing our relationship with nature, spending time connecting with its beauty as a way to gain insight, and using it to recharge our internal batteries. If I ever needed recharging, it was now!

For eight days I absorbed the wonder and beauty of unspoiled Alaska. No swimming, no cycling and no running. This was my final chance before Kona to develop the inner strength necessary to deflect the inevitable onslaught of the world's best—younger athletes ready to knock me off the top. Brant helped me regain a lot of the energy I'd expended in the previous years. He talked through ancient wisdom directed at fortifying the parts of my inner character that we all have in common and that we can all use to create positive change within ourselves. "Quiet brings awareness, answers. Joy washes away negativity. Trust replaces doubt. Gratitude calms our heart and brings renewed hope. Laughter is healing. Connect with nature and you connect with your heart, with purpose." These simple concepts can give you a fighting chance in life.

Our greatest assets are seldom possessions. Computers are certainly useful. Cars essential. Homes can be a place of solace and comfort. But it's our character, our inner makeup that defines the outcome and quality of our existence. Creativity activates innovation. Commitment keeps our thirst for immediate results at bay. Calm silences the static of negativity. Developing these timeless resources, essentials for creating art through our actions, can best be cultivated away from the arena where they will have the biggest and most profound impact. It's tough to develop calm during a track workout when pain is the main feature. But having the track workout of your life is made possible when you have already developed the ability to dial up calm and can place it front and center during the intensity of that moment.

Brant was helping me with all those necessary elements. But there was still something nagging me, like an ever-present alarm sounding its relentless warning. Just before leaving for Alaska, I had received the results of a blood test measuring the overall state of my body. The outcome was paralyzing: Every hormone necessary for peak functioning as a top athlete was depleted. By the lab results I looked like I was closer to sixty-seven than thirty-seven. The only remedies offered from the medical professionals were illegal from a competitive standpoint. Art and cheating do not intersect! There had to be another way. I asked Brant for help.

He worked intensively to bring all my markers up. Brant is a shaman and healer, an Indian doctor who works through song, adjusting a patient's energy with prayer and arranging good health with his ceremonies. It defies modern-day reality to think about a song bringing up your testosterone levels, but in the ancient tradition of the Huichols, it's as ordinary and accepted a practice of healing as taking an antibiotic would be in the modern world.

OCTOBER 7, 1995

This was it. My final Ironman. I did everything within my power to prepare. I'd cut out even more of my training to help my body recover. The longest and toughest days still got logged, but the fluff was completely eliminated. Brant's work and his words had succeeded in fortifying both mind and body. I felt as good as could be expected race morning. "Nervous" is a positive energy if contained and regulated. I had it just where it needed to be. I saw only one possibility as the outcome of the day, that I would accomplish my goal.

Being aware of the places you might be called to in the pivotal moments of intense competition is normally unnerving. But this year was different. They didn't dizzy my mind. They brought me a sense of calm. I'd been there before and survived. This would be no different.

Ten minutes to the start and I felt a peace like no other time in Kona. Acceptance of the task ahead was powerful.

Unbeknownst to me a silent pact had been made among my competitors. One-on-one they didn't feel they had a chance. All-against-one and the cards were in their favor. My clear advantage in the race had been endurance. In short, I had more left in the tank for the marathon than just about anyone and could patiently dose my effort throughout the day, waiting, watching, moving up through the field gradually, applying the pressure until only one would remain and then none. It always happened during the marathon, and rarely before the final hour of the race. Neutralizing my weapon with a blistering pace in the swim and on the bike was their code. Set a speed so fast that I would have nothing left for the run if I were to match it, or leave me so far behind that I would have absolutely no hope of closing the gap they would open.

The Art of Competition knows struggle. It gives it full embrace. Art is born from the far reaches of uncertainty and impossibility, when only something that is one-of-a-kind, that has never before taken form, is being called forth. It is not a high or a low. Art demands both be treated with equal indifference. Only then can Art's midpoint for crafting greatness be engaged fully and completely without distraction.

Unfortunately, the real world can make this a tough template to follow. So can your competitors. The collective "them" had devised a brilliant plan, and it was working. After the swim and the bike, I began my final Ironman marathon in fifth place, thirteen and a half minutes behind the leader, an upstart German athlete named Thomas Hellriegel. He was out of sight, which was a huge disadvantage for me. He could have bad patches and I would never know about them or be able to capitalize on them. To me it would seem like he was running unwaveringly; he had a two-mile head start. Thirteen years my junior, he had opened a chasm no one had ever successfully closed to gain the crown. Logic saw only impossibility.

The first steps of the marathon felt futile, the next ones even more so. Fourteen years of triathlon racing gave me no clear strategy of how I could pull this off. Confidence was replaced with cynicism, and then the simple idea to just quit. My internal chatter was corrosive. Not one word I was thinking was helping.

The Art of Competition allows you to come up with the ideas, the solutions, the ways of going forward that never present themselves through logic. It relieves the outcome of being important and bestows the highest significance to the exact moment at hand. Nothing else matters. That focus quiets your mind. Art begins the instant stillness is initiated. Every facet of your being opens up, locks in and ignites the potential just waiting to be catalyzed in that moment, and then the next. Past and future disappear. Winning and losing are forgotten. You've let the others take care of competing. You are the guardian of Art. The only possibility is that anything is possible.

A mile later I was just steps shy of the greatest excuse my cynical mind had seen to quit: the driveway to my hotel. I slipped into silence. It took a quick moment in that precious state to contemplate if I was really going to just call it a career and careen down that tempting path to a quiet air-conditioned hotel room. But instead of a resolved decision, it was Brant's words that marched forward in that short sliver of quiet and catapulted me back into the race: "It's not over until it's over. Give it everything you have and trust."

That became my mantra. Give it everything and trust. That is what Art requires. A quarter of a mile later I made the first pass of a competitor in front of me moving from fifth place to fourth. Two miles after that I had worked my way into third. By the half marathon point, thirteen miles left in my Ironman career, I slid into second. Still out of sight, Hellriegel ran ahead. His presence and his lead were written all over the faces of the spectators who were looking incredulously at their watches figuring out the time gap between us. With eight miles to go a bystander shouted out that I was four minutes behind the German.

For nearly two hours of running I'd been locked into that wonderful artful place of racing where inside I was silent. But that discouraging bit of information sideswiped me and dragged me back into the world of thinking and analyzing. Time is only meaningful if you go by its measure and can only be detrimental if you fall prey to its predictions. I made the mistake of doing a quick calculation. I had been closing the gap on Hellriegel at a rate of nearly thirty seconds per mile. At my current tempo, with the distance left and the gap still looming large between Hellriegel and me, I'd catch him just short of the finish line, just shy of victory.

Impossibility forces the choice between accepting defeat and creating Art. If you choose Art there still is no guarantee that the outcome will be what you had originally intended. But it is a good choice because no matter how the ending is written, the story will then be priceless!

I had less than fifty minutes of racing left to do the impossible and win a sixth Ironman World Title in six starts. It took Dave Scott eight races to amass his six victories. Only one competitor stood between me and my being crowned the oldest men's champion to date. A gap of four minutes was keeping "the greatest comeback in Ironman history" from being forever attached to my name. But the collective force levied against me by of the rest of the field was devastating. It had demanded a steadiness in my marathon that allowed for no mistake, no miscalculation that would leave me shy of running the entire 26.2 miles faster than every other competitor in the race. I needed something more but was starting to feel I would never find it. Amazingly in the next moment I realized that the "something" I needed was standing ever-present all around me.

The Big Island of Hawaii is one of the jewels in Nature's treasure chest. It sits surrounded by more blue ocean than any other landmass on the planet. Its highest mountain, a dormant volcanic wonder named Mauna Kea, if measured from its base at the ocean's floor all the way up to its peak has a height that is nearly 4,000 feet taller than Mt. Everest. Brant said, "If you need help call out to the Island. It will hear you and help you."

Art defies the explainable. I called out. "Help me Big Island. I'm going to give it everything I have, but I need your help." In the next mile the gap between my unseen competitor and me shrank by forty seconds. The one after that it closed by nearly fifty, and the one after that I gnawed another minute and fifteen seconds out of Hellriegel's cushion. At mile twenty of the marathon, I caught the first sight of Hellriegel since he'd passed me earlier on the bike.

As mile twenty-three approached, the gap between us was so slight that if I had called out his name he would have heard me. I slowed my approach, letting the distance between us stay static to give me one final moment of regrouping. The effort had been immense and I needed a second to actually assess my reserves.

Being smart is also involved with creating art in competition. If I was nearing the end of my energy reserves, it could be best to carry the momentum I had built and pass him immediately in the hope that he, too, was clinging to a pace with a price. If there were more than a few vapors left in my tank, I could use that luxury to run behind him for a moment and try to assess his state before making a decisive and determined move. Maybe I could even wait until we approached the same hill where my first victory six years earlier was forged!

The Art of Competition necessitates embracing uncertainty rather than being paralyzed by it. There can be many solutions that flood the scene, but which is the best? Uncertainty doesn't care. It simply asks you to choose one and commit. I was uncertain. Just over three miles to go in an Ironman marathon feels like walking across the surface of the moon. More collapses have happened and dreams broken in that final countdown to the finish than at any other singular place on the course. I knew that. A wrong move in those closing miles and your day could be shut down with severe cramps. Or you might be forced to slow to a crawl because you burned all your matches to shake a relentless competitor too early. Embrace uncertainty. Make a choice and commit. I had to do that. I could not tell if I had enough reserve to wait or if it was best to try to play my hand immediately. What's the answer?

Art is born out of silence. I quieted my mind, stopped looking for the solution, and waited to see if it would present itself. Logic saw no great strategy. I waited, running just steps behind Hellriegel for what seemed to be miles but in reality was only a handful of seconds.

It was time. I surged, pulling even and then ahead. The smallest of gaps was now in my favor. I had it! But then Hellriegel answered back. He clung to my shoulder. The alarms sounded. "He's just toying with me. He's got a lot left. He was just resting, waiting for me to catch him so he could assess me. Now he's going to make the decisive move."

Embrace uncertainty and commit. I held pace, and then it really happened. Thomas slowly slipped back, one step then two, then more until he was out of my vision. He'd answered with one last unnerving salute, with every ounce of energy he had left. That became the final pass of my Ironman career. Fifteen minutes later I crossed the Ironman finish line, for the final time, just over two minutes ahead of this unyielding competitor. In the process I completed the greatest race of my career.

The television broadcast two months later could never show the tireless string of moments when I wanted to quit. The audience was unaware of how many times five victories sounded like enough or the countless other times when the struggle to rein this one in just didn't seem worth it. You never saw them because each and every one succumbed to the unyielding pressure applied by steadiness. You never heard the constant revival of my internal chatter that had nothing good to say until the race was complete because those damaging thoughts were muffled, then fell silent under the force of a trust that was called up and had the final sway in the outcome.

Art is born out of the impossible. This final Ironman victory was truly an impossible one, but the prize had been won long before the race was over. The toughest battles are never seen. The greatest victories are the ones over yourself. Ironman, Hellriegel, my other competitors all demanded I win those battles and find that greatest victory as my answer to their challenge. It truly was The Art of Competition.

CHAPTER 10: REALIZE

THE ART OF COMPETITION

180

APPARENT EASE IS THE WEAPON
OF A CHAMPION.

THE ART OF COMPETITION

THE ART OF COMPETITION

182

GREATNESS BEGINS
ONCE THE BATTLE IS DONE.

A RESULT CAN ONLY BE BAD IF ONE
DOES NOT LEARN FROM IT.

THE ART OF COMPETITION

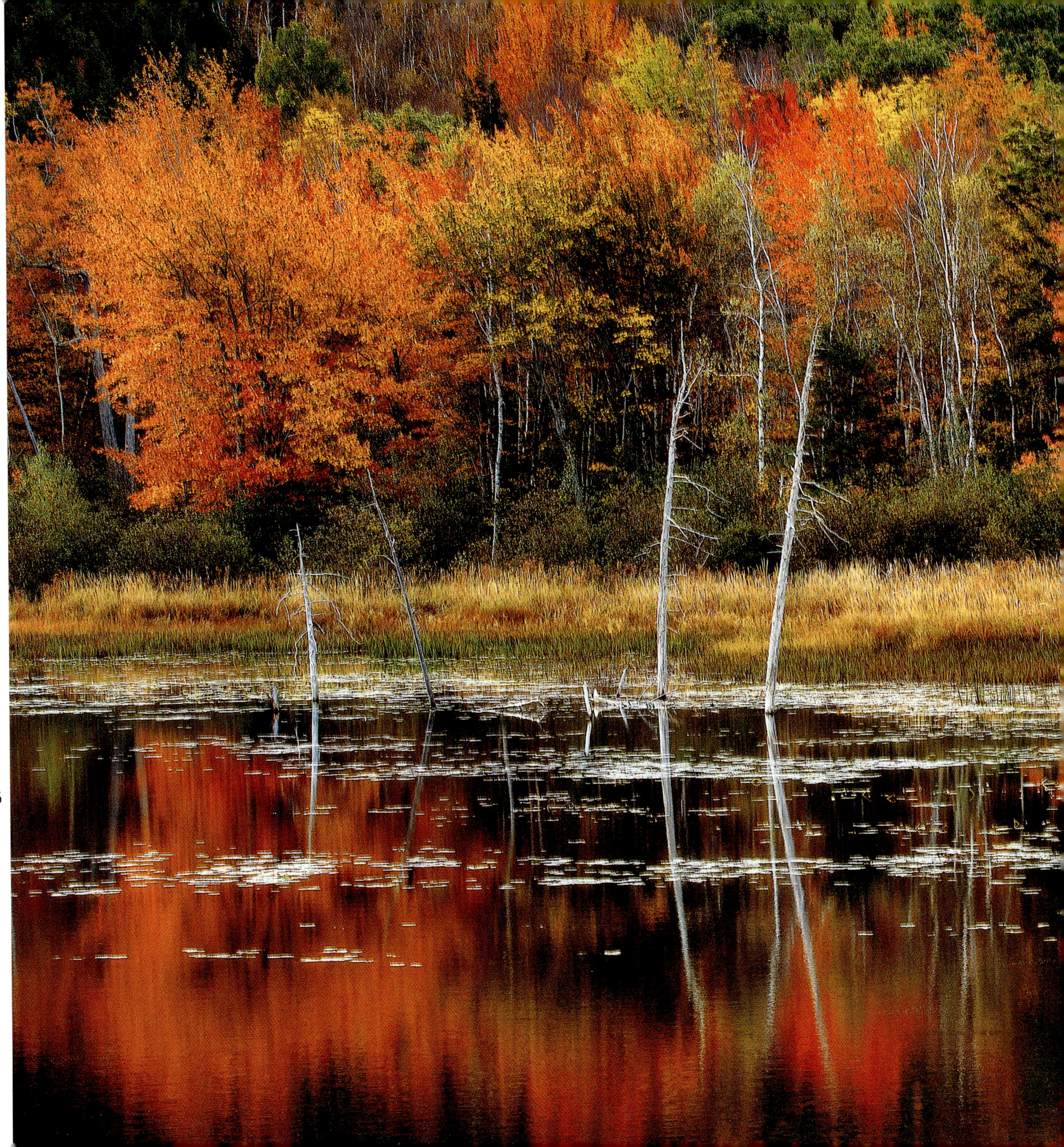

REGROUPING IS NOT GIVING UP.

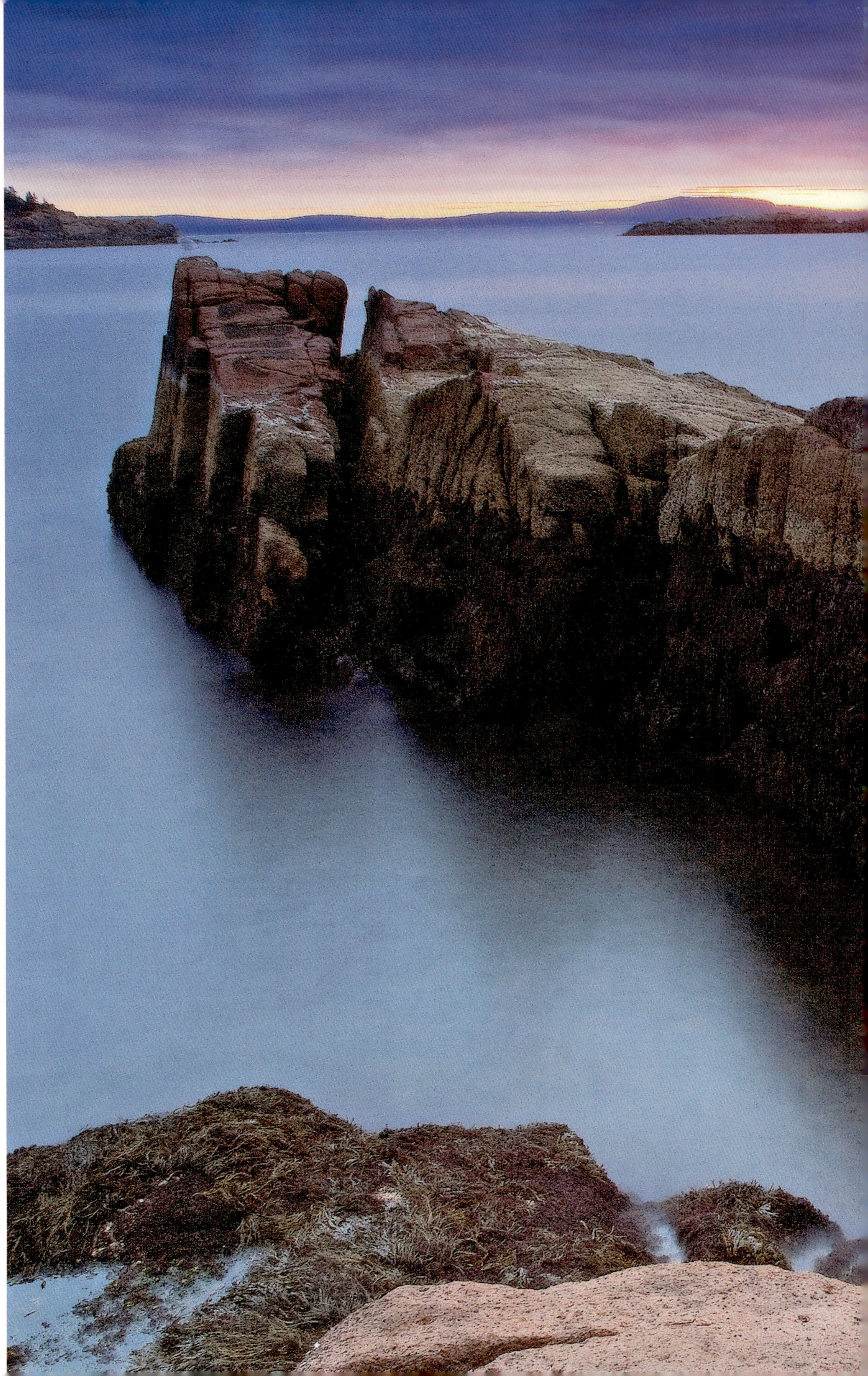

THE WINNER IS THE FIRST TO FINISH;
EVERYTHING BEFORE THAT IS FORGOTTEN.

THE ART OF COMPETITION

190

HUMILITY ERASES DEFEAT.

THE ART OF COMPETITION

SELF-CONFIDENCE DOES NOT EXIST
IN A THOUGHT; IT IS HOUSED IN SILENCE.
STOP THINKING AND YOU WILL FIND IT.

THE ART OF COMPETITION

194

THAT WHICH ENDURES TIME GIVES ONE
STRENGTH IN THE MOMENT.

THE ART OF COMPETITION

196

THE FINAL STEP IS POSSIBLE ONLY BECAUSE OF THE THOUSANDS TAKEN BEFORE IT.

THE ART OF COMPETITION

197

VICTORY OVER ANOTHER IS FLEETING;
VICTORY OVER ONESELF IS ENDURING.

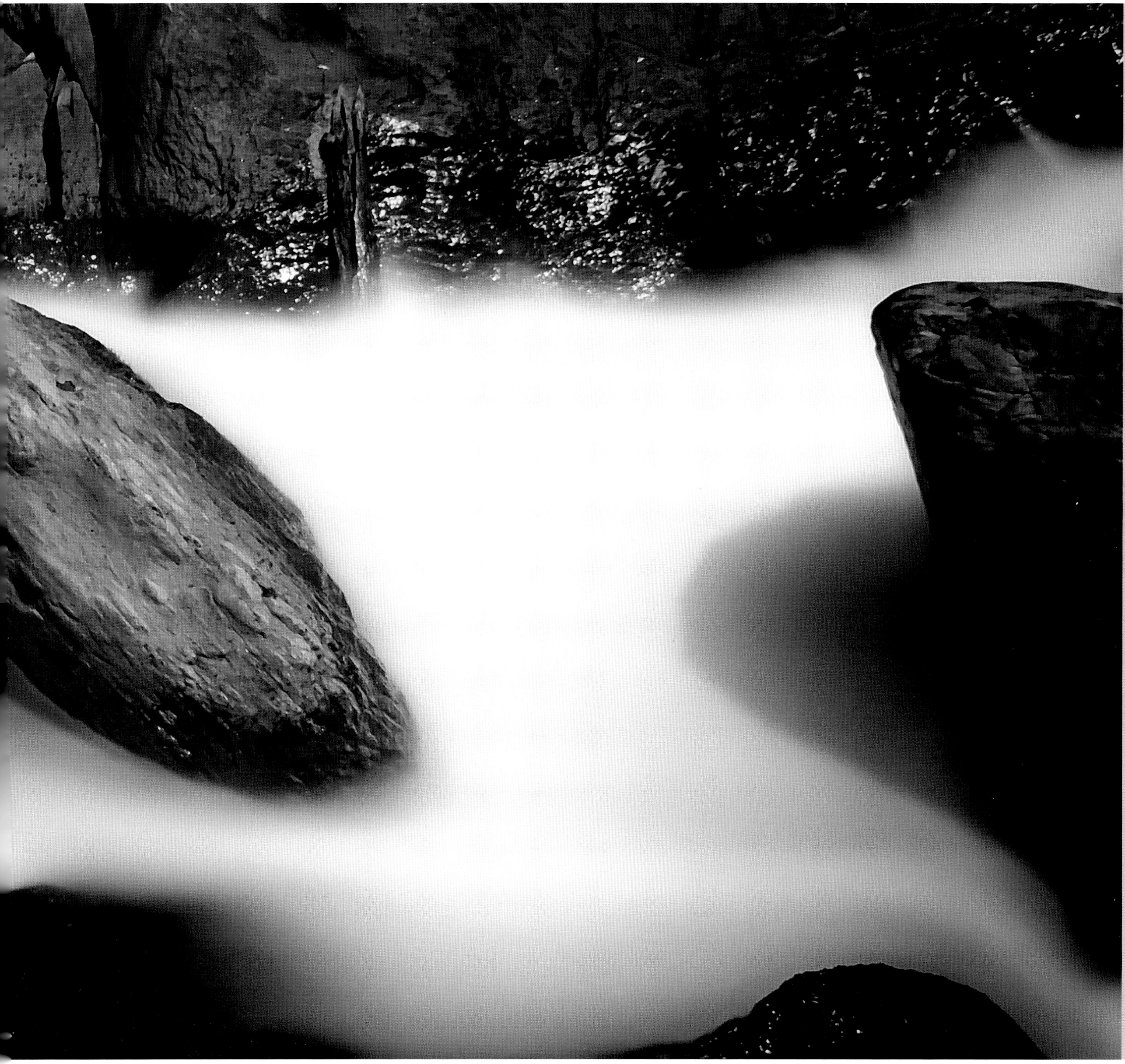

THE ART OF COMPETITION

200

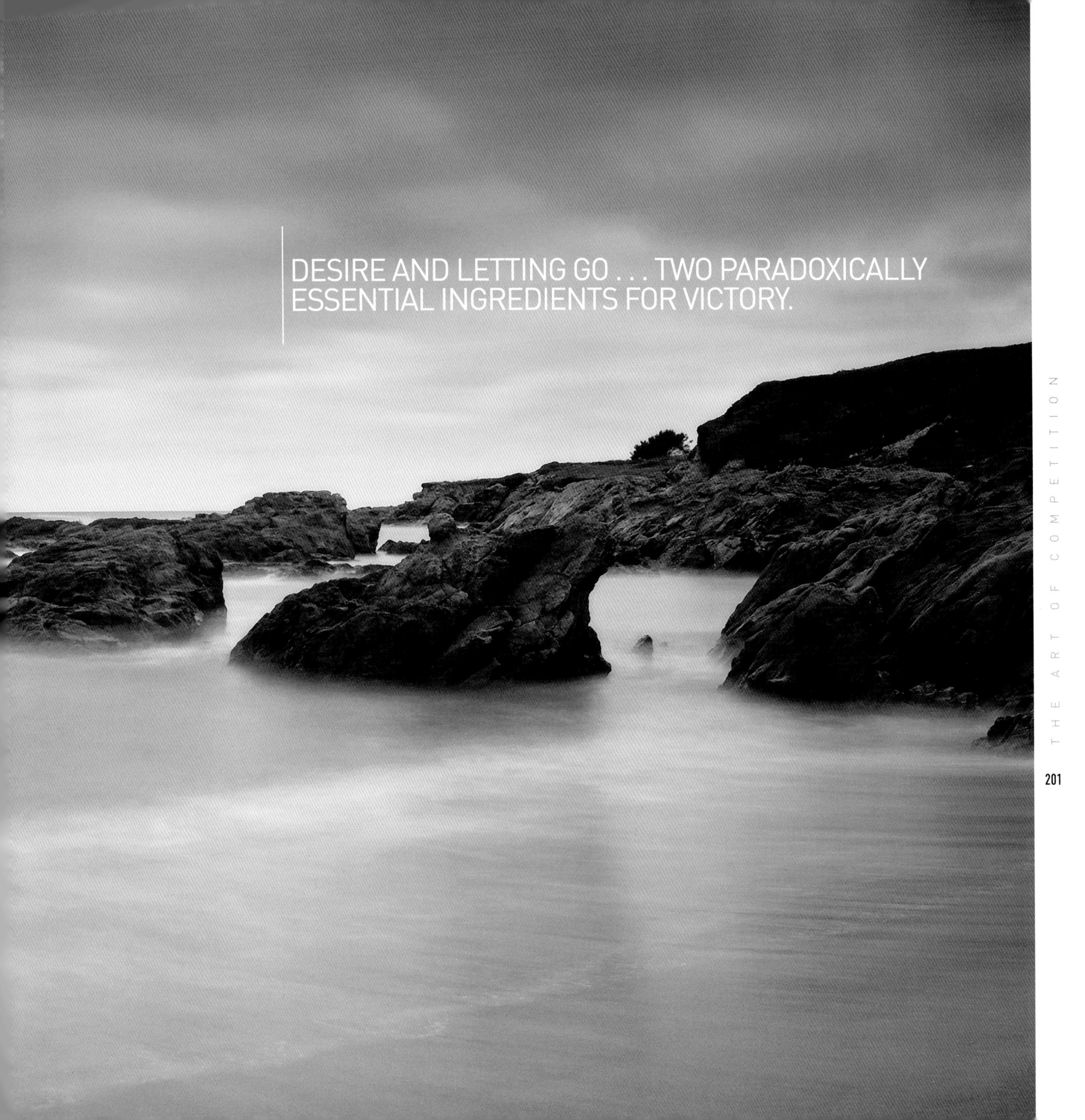

DESIRE AND LETTING GO . . . TWO PARADOXICALLY ESSENTIAL INGREDIENTS FOR VICTORY.

THE ART OF COMPETITION

202

EXCELLENCE HAS LITTLE TIME FOR DOUBT.

THE ART OF COMPETITION

203

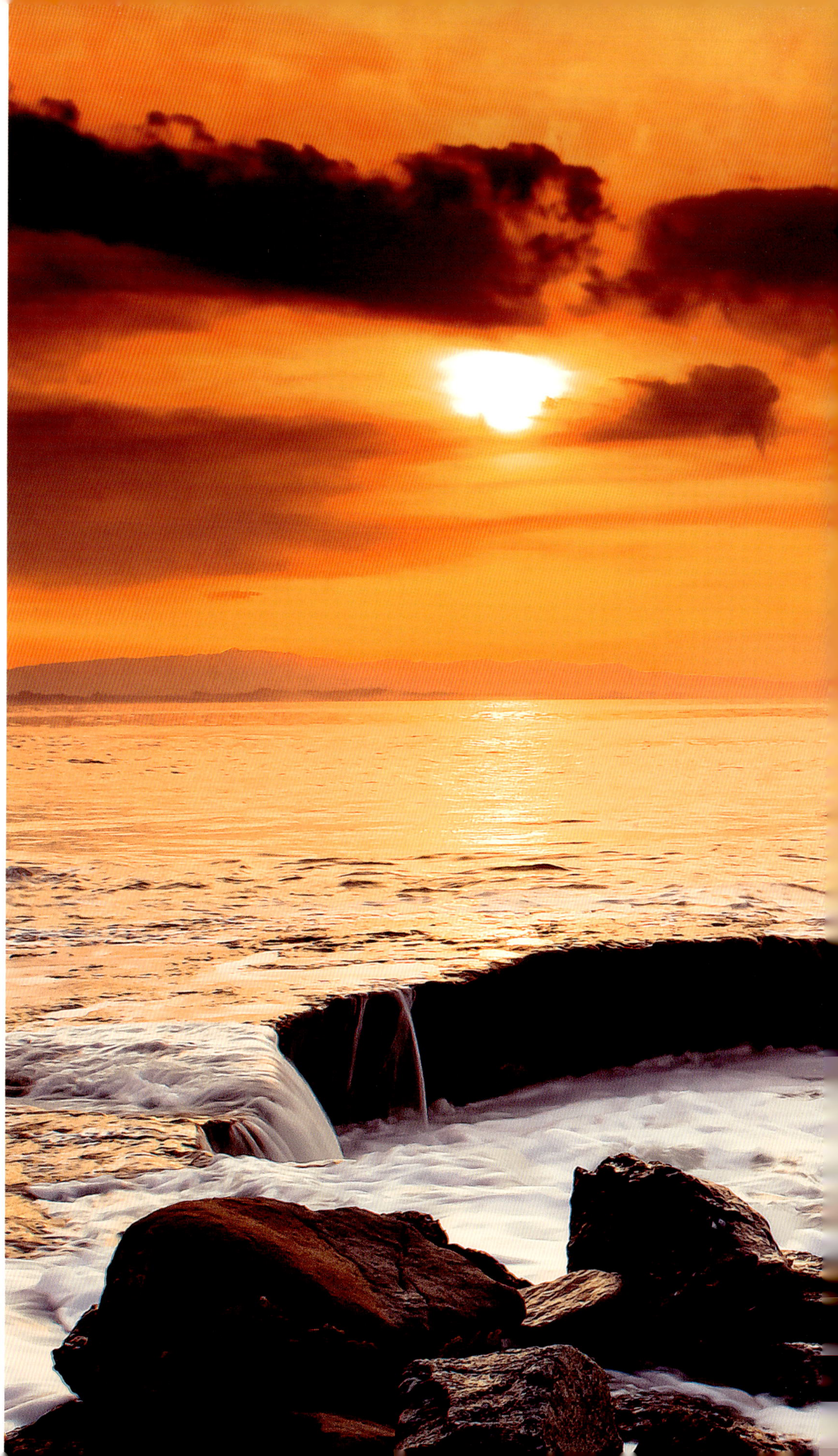

| CHALLENGE IS A TEST OF COMMITMENT.

THE ART OF COMPETITION

SILENCE IS THE MOST POTENT RESPONSE TO CHALLENGE AND WILL TAKE YOU PAST IT EVERY TIME.

EXCELLENCE IS ONLY RECOGNIZABLE ONCE IT IS OVER; YOU NEVER SEE IT IN THE MOMENT.

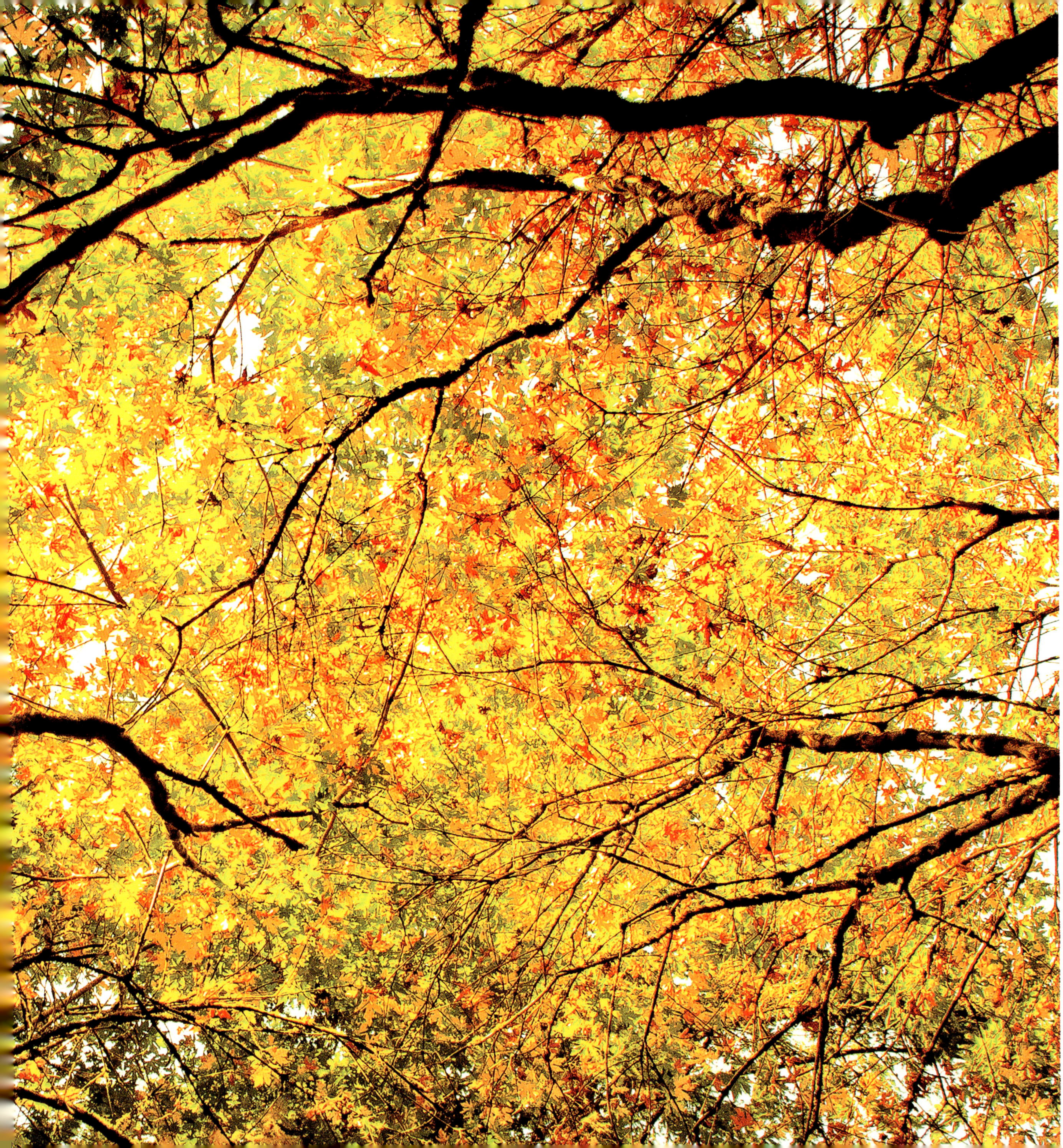

FOCUS IS EVER-CHANGING WHEN FOLLOWING A TARGET.
EXCELLENCE IS A MOVING TARGET.

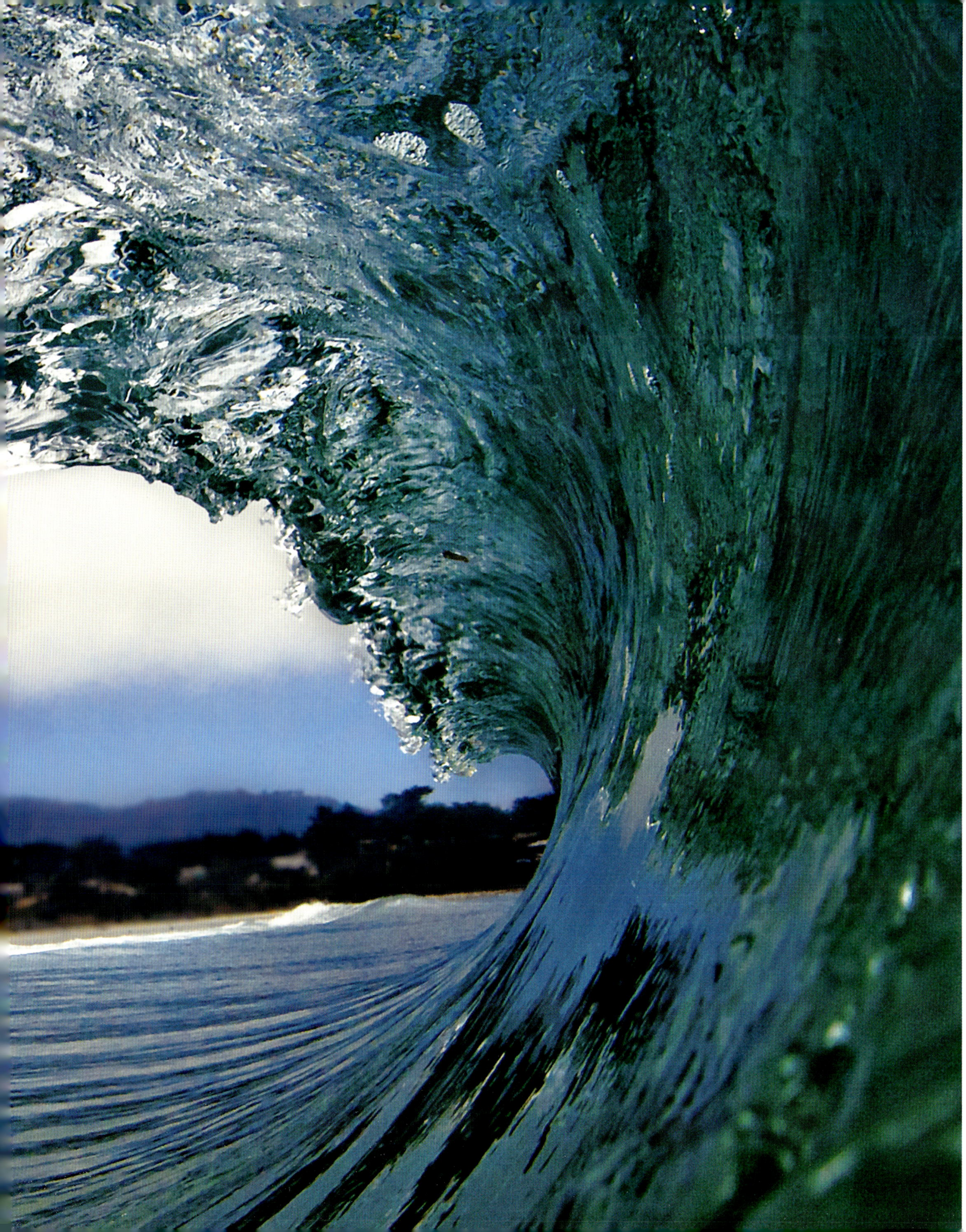

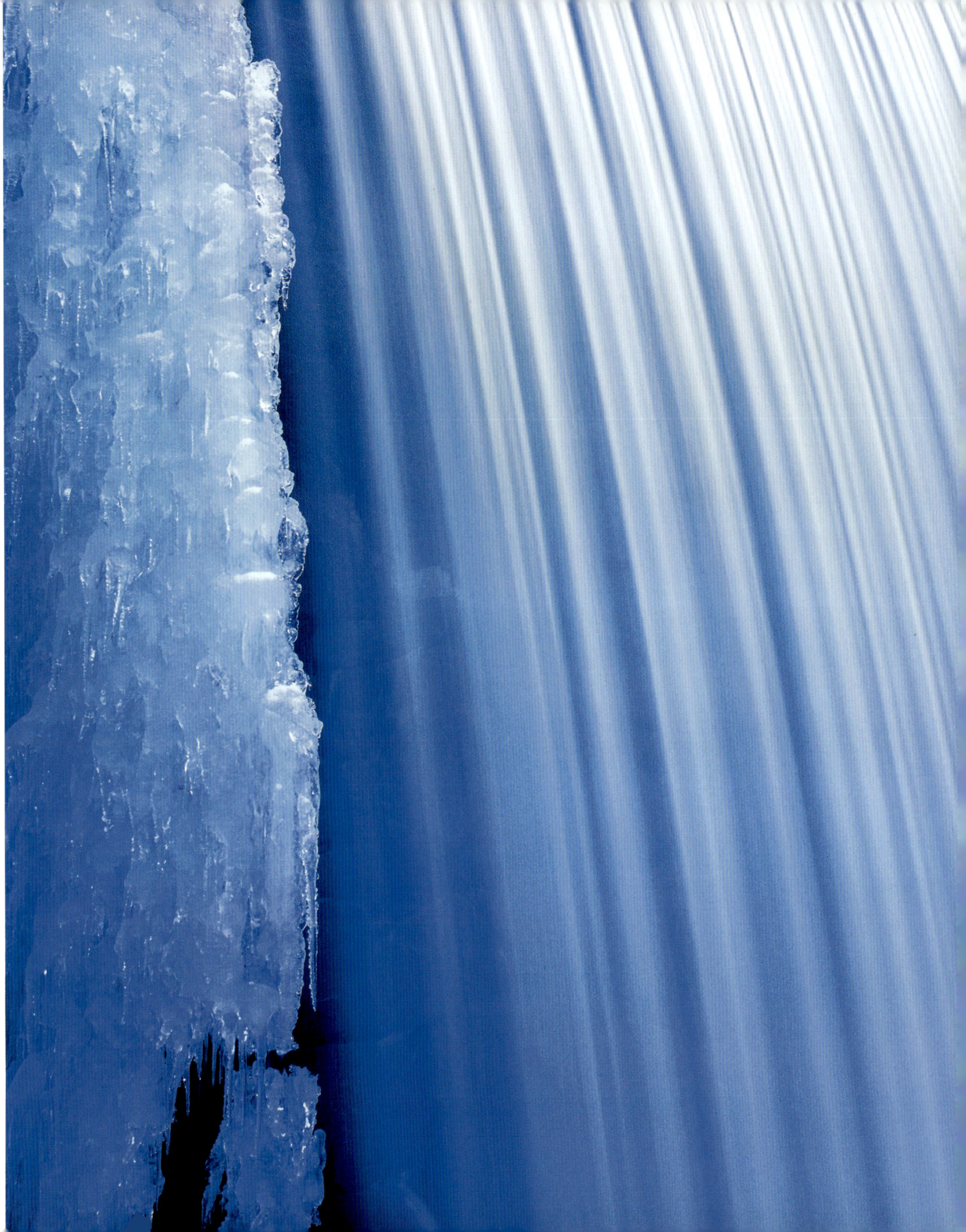

LIFE IS A PRAYER.

THE ART OF COMPETITION

213

WHEN ALL ELSE FAILS, **OPEN A CAN OF WHOOP-ASS AND TAKE A BIG LONG SIP.**

LIMITED EDITION

Photos by:
Mark Allen, Mats Allen and Nico Secunda

THE ART OF COMPETITION

PERFECTION DEMANDS...

This is the first quote in the book and it sets the stage. It speaks directly to the exactitude of perfection, that it's not a free ride. Without being said directly, it wipes away all the sugarcoated promises about greatness and puts it front and center that those seeking the highest level of excellence will be required to step up. These two words say that the experience cannot be bought or bargained for; it's not owed you because of anything you may have done in the past or just because you feel it's your right in the future.

The word "demand" clearly braces you for the work ahead. It suggests a road that could be uncomfortable, that will likely be testing your commitment. "Demand" implies that you are not going to be in charge of the journey. Athletic perfection is going to demand a state of steadfastness focusing on the goal and will likely test you with endless exit ramps trying to weaken your commitment to completion. Rise up before the first step is taken, then hold on!

But there's another side to this quote. It's the dot, dot, dot. Those three symbols are the personalization of the pursuit. What demands there are will be different for each person, and change for each quest of perfection you search for. There is no set formula, and likely many of the demands will be unexpected, iconic in proportion, and sometimes as elusive and invisible to answer as the empty space that follows those three dots on this page.

This is the element that transforms the endeavor into Art. A defined recipe for success will lead you to the border of Art. Entering its zone requires finding out what lies beyond the dot, dot, dot. Discovery is the easy way to say it. Take a step toward your vision, then the next. Start moving in the right direction until the road of predictability ends and you must take a leap toward the next foothold, even if it's not in focus until you are midair with no way back. That's when you'll understand what perfection demands.

A CHAMPION EXPLOITS EVERY DETAIL WITHOUT EVER FORGETTING THE BASICS.

There is almost endless possibility when it comes to the avenues an athlete can exploit to be better at their craft: exotic training techniques, nutritional extracts and extremes, unusual recovery therapies and a ceaseless search for equipment that will give the greatest advantage. They all make up the niceties that promise for a better day of competition experience.

Proceed with caution, however. Amassing layer upon layer of extras, each of which might seem essential at first glance, can collapse the entire dream with what I call "detail exhaustion." Managing all the secret advantages that you are sure will be the tipping point for success can leave you with only half a tank to take care of the core, truly essential elements that are the main obligation for performance. That basket of basics must be solid before it gets refined and honed with the trimmings.

Here's a simple example of the basics from the world of triathlon. It goes without saying that a triathlete has to be able to swim, bike and run, and do them all at a fairly high level. Those are the core basics that create a foundation for performance, the elements that must never be forgotten. After those are covered a second level of details usually evolves that seems just as essential. These could include diet, sleep, mindset, equipment upgrades and injury prevention. Never compromise the development of the basics at the expense of adding in more facets. You may be able to run an hour faster in an Ironman with better training. You might gain a minute with a different pair of running shoes. Both are good. One must never be forgotten.

Gradually expand your tools to integrate beyond the basics, and continue to build as long as the expansion is helping. But never rely on these extra details to prop up weaknesses in the basic tool kit. Knowing the difference between basics and add-ons is the art of a champion.

A RACE IS TRUTH IN MOTION.

We all have our dream days scored out on the landscape of our mind. We see how it's going to unfold, where the hiccups might come along the way, and the strategies that will take us past them. We take stock of the work that has gotten us to the gateway of truth, where one side is our past preparation and the other the potential to fulfill our dreams.

The moment of crossing over could be the starting cannon of the biggest race of your life. It might come from your name being called out as the next person to perform a routine, the ending of the national anthem that signals it's time to play. Whatever it is, your moment is at hand. And the second the action starts, truth takes over!

That truth can be a real and clear understanding of the immensity your challenge holds. It can be the skill of a challenger who's going to require your best game if you want to make the grade. The truth will always come from focusing on the deepest recesses of your character, asking each and every hidden corner if you are really willing to lock in and engage, no matter what. You will see if you've prepared correctly, and if you didn't, truth will force you to forge a different strategy for success that has nothing to do with ideal.

A race, a game, a match are all truth in motion. It won't be just one signpost with your name written on it. There will be hundreds where truth must be faced between the starting gun and the final finish, even in the shortest of contests. Knowing truth is coming before the test is the unnerving part. It's unknown, uncertain. It raises the question, "What will I have to see today?" It's settling when you actually get a chance to meet it head on, when you get to dissolve the fantasy of a competition and rise up to its reality. The Art is in the embrace. Yes it's tough; the situation can look impossible. You might see your weakness, but Art doesn't really care about all that. You are there for one purpose, to embrace the potential of the moment offered. That is also truth . . . that anything indeed is possible, even in the face of the most unlikely odds. Embrace it. Become it.

INNER PEACE, THEN OUTER RESULTS: NOT THE OTHER WAY AROUND.

The meaning of this quote can be very effective if embraced purely on face value. It's saying to find a place inside yourself that is peaceful and fulfilled before you put on your working gloves and set out to create something of meaning.

What are you hunting for? If it becomes yours, you likely see that it will indeed bring you contentment. Whatever it is, it will come your way more easily, with less effort and more certainty, if that final peace you seek is found before you toe the line. Find that end happiness before you start. Feel satisfied before the race rather than waiting until the results are tallied to see if you matched a level you would call successful, fulfilling or worth the effort. That's one way of applying this quote.

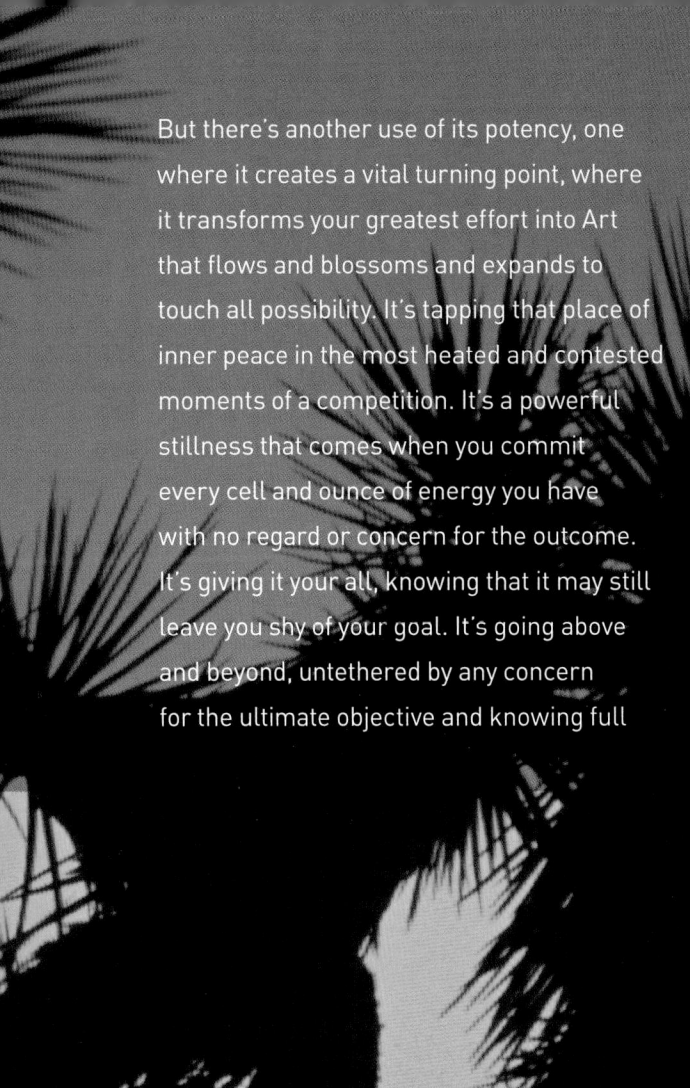

But there's another use of its potency, one where it creates a vital turning point, where it transforms your greatest effort into Art that flows and blossoms and expands to touch all possibility. It's tapping that place of inner peace in the most heated and contested moments of a competition. It's a powerful stillness that comes when you commit every cell and ounce of energy you have with no regard or concern for the outcome. It's giving it your all, knowing that it may still leave you shy of your goal. It's going above and beyond, untethered by any concern for the ultimate objective and knowing full well that it could just as easily lead to total collapse as it could to unparalleled success. It's peace in action. It has no need for the final result to justify the effort. The engagement is the reward, the immediate moment of complete commitment the purpose. However it turns out is secondary because the gap has been closed between wanting to succeed and succeeding. It's been filled with something greater than any end result can bring. You have peace, and it will be there the second your forces gather and focus on the instant at hand, then the next. This is Art. This is how the greats step up to excellence.

PERFECTION HAS ITS OWN SILENCE FILLED WITH ALL YOU NEED.

I love the clutch moments in sports. You can probably picture a few that are forever etched in your own mind. It could be a quarterback releasing the ball to a receiver in the end zone, neither really knowing whether the play will end in a score that brings victory. Perhaps it was a gymnast needing to stick the final dismount. The eternity of spinning through air can be intense, because it would all mean nothing if the meeting of feet with mat is anything other than completely solid. What was going on in the stands at that pivotal moment? There might have been a breath-holding silence while everyone waited, watching through the lens of anticipation as time slowed. It could have been deafeningly loud, with everyone on their feet cheering, willing the outcome with their cries.

Whatever the scene of those watching, one thing is for sure: there was silence inside the competitor at that moment of athletic imminence. It started the instant the final effort was initiated, and it carried through until its full execution was completed. That is the only way perfection exists. Thinking gets in the way. Desire slows down its trajectory. Worrying about the outcome while in the middle of creating it bears an invisible weight that keeps the dream from flying to its necessary height.

In the silence of perfection, everything that is needed exists: the will, the force, the skill and coordination. In that silence is the answer to impossibility. It is there that one finds the self-confidence to give it more than you would be capable of at any other moment in life. It's perfection of the highest order because it brings forth a person's absolute top performance, one that inspires and is worthy of the cheers going on all around them. The instant stillness sets in you stop trying to come up with a clutch move and just become the vehicle to bring its perfection forth.

DESIRE PUTS YOU WITHIN SIGHT OF GREATNESS. SURRENDER ENABLES YOU TO EMBRACE IT.

Call it desire and passion or the intrigue at solving a puzzle that has no immediate answer: these are the reasons someone might devote a very large portion of their waking hours to pursuing a big goal.

The more of your capabilities the goal requires, the more time and energy you must expend to reach it. We all know this.

Likely there will be a lot of repetition in one form or another that builds the foundation for accomplishing the dream. Then there's a whole lot more of the same that will get you within sniffing distance of its intoxicating aroma. We all know this, too.

That great desire to achieve, to fulfill your grand destiny, is the magnetic force pulling you in the direction through the months, even years, of preparation necessary to realize your aspirations. That yearning helps you avoid lethal distractions that could derail your morale and make you throw in the towel just inches shy of crossing that final threshold separating you from greatness.

But that final point needed to take the lead, the last pass of a competitor that has held you off until both of you are in sight of the finish, a critical last move you must accomplish flawlessly to accumulate the points needed for victory all require something very different than desire. They require surrender.

Desire needs the potential of fulfillment to survive. It takes energy to hold onto it. Surrender requires none. It's that state within Art where one fully embraces all the possibility that the next moment holds, both the greatness of success and the potential to come up short. Surrender looks at both as secondary, as distractions that sap your focus and keep you from fully locking into the task at hand.

Surrender allows full embrace, full engagement. The ball gets released, the surge to pass is initiated, a move riddled with potential disaster is performed. When done with surrender, with no concern of the outcome, the full force of your character can take charge. Embracing all outcomes makes that moment yours. It takes you into the greatness you dreamed of.

EXCELLENCE HAS LITTLE TIME FOR DOUBT.

Doubt is an emotion everyone has experienced at some point in their life. It can be very small, so insignificant that it's just annoying background static that has no effect on your focus; you stay dialed into the task at hand regardless. Other times it can be the only thing you hear. It distracts us. It drains our energy, pops the balloon holding our motivation. It might even stop us in our tracks while we try to figure out how to deal with the failure rather than taking the one step that will move us closer to achieving our dreams. If the journey had meaning when you started, something that called to you from deep down inside, there is no room for crippling doubt in your pursuit of excellence. It's time to call on that greater part of yourself and get it to rise up.

That can be a tough order to fill when doubt is in the equation. Doubt has its own undeniable weight and mass. It slows reaction time. It clouds focus. It tightens muscles and stifles creativity.

But doubt can be dealt a debilitating blow. It starts by rededicating your efforts and giving it all that you have in the moment at hand. It fizzles with a simple thought—"I don't have to be feeling one hundred percent to give one hundred percent of what I have right now."

Doubt becomes a distant echo when we embrace the possibility that things can turn around in the next instant, and if not then, in the one that follows. It disappears completely when we trust that however the final chapter of the day gets written life will still be worth living. That is excellence. That is what turns Competition into Art in the moments when doubt could have had the final word.

DISCIPLINE IS FLEXIBLE.

In the big pursuits there is usually not a whole lot of need to drum up motivation. The goal, the dream, has its own magnetism, drawing its holder into action day after day. To those on the outside it looks like unwavering discipline, an image of working hard and long toward the goal with a commitment that never seems to bend.

But those walking the big journeys know it's not that clear cut. There are cycles and changes in rhythm to every pursuit. Some days we have the strength, energy and insight to keep up with the ideal strategy that we set in play. Other times there is absolutely no hope of matching anything close to that standard. These are the moments when true Art allows for flexibility, for the sometimes small, and occasionally big, adaptations that need to be overlaid on the greatest of intentions. Flexibility keeps "discipline" from turning into an oppressive and unhealthy obligation capable of strangling the vibrancy that training and working toward a goal should bring.

The human body and mind are dynamic systems, not information systems. No one on the planet can simply program a year's worth of preparation and have it match the ups and downs of energy levels and motivation that inevitably wax and wane endlessly over time. One must be willing to apply some flex. A game plan can never incorporate the immeasurable number of real-world variables that affect our ability to train and perform. Flexibility is essential to making sure one backs off just enough when a necessary alteration of plans surfaces, so that it doesn't become a breaking point. Discipline is essential. Rigid discipline is oppressive.

The catch, or the Art, is in figuring out when to be methodical and when to be flexible. Repetition is the bread and butter of great performances. Without it no one can master their sport. But it can be boring. It can become wearing. Too much and there is nothing left for the day of the race, the game or the match. A competitor becomes an artist when they are capable of distinguishing which valued trait must be followed on any given day. Should I be disciplined? Or should I be flexible? Which will get me one step closer to the dream I have for myself? By asking the question, the answer will come!

EASY CHANGES RARELY LEAD TO VICTORY.

Human nature can be generally lazy. It's a strategy for survival that enables the maximum results to come from the least amount of work. That's not necessarily a negative trait. Conserving precious energy in ancient times when grocery stores didn't line the tundra provided a strategy for existence that allowed hunting just far and wide enough to live in periods of scarcity. Times have changed though, and in fact most of us in the modern world would probably gain some long overdue breathing room if we incorporated even a small dose of laziness into our weekly routine! However, when we embark on a journey to fulfill a big dream, a big calling, there will come a moment when we are asked to make a change that is at the other extreme from easy or lazy. It will be a change in behavior, a different way of doing things that takes us so far outside of any zone we would call comfortable or familiar that it can feel like we are doing something akin to facing death. But if this one change is essential to the success we are after, it will also be worth tackling. Slay the beast and raise the victory flag over your personal fear of going head to head with a reworking of your inner approach. Then you can claim victory, a personal best, a supreme performance called Art. It's available once you commit and then act on this key change in training, in focus, in how you respond to the impossible and the improbable.

Many champions never make the difficult changes. They came into this world with enough raw talent to go far. They had the good luck to be guided by coaches and mentors who helped them hone those natural gifts. But even these elite, the supremely gifted, must at some point embrace difficult changes in their approach if they are going to outlast, outperform and outfox a less talented opponent who has done the hard work. Without it their less endowed foe is going to ride the momentum of their work above and beyond their reluctant talented adversary who hasn't.

To help bring this quote more focus directly to your life let me ask you a simple question: what is one thing that you know is essential to your success that you have been avoiding doing because it is uncomfortable, uncertain or unfamiliar? Think about it for a moment. You likely already know the answer, but if not, reflect. Do you have it? Now's the time! Commit to that change. Make it a go-to behavior, a way of approaching your quest for the next six weeks. By then it will be part of your DNA, and a quality you can count on in your pursuit of Art.

EVEN CHAMPIONS STRUGGLE.

When things are tough we can think that everyone else has it smooth, that it's just us struggling. This thought can be especially true in competition when a rival pulls ahead then out of reach with apparent ease. Indeed at that precise point in time your assessment could be correct. It could be that they are feeling great and that you are the only one struggling. But you never know what tests they had to pass in the moments before or what will come their way in the moments to follow. Even champions struggle!

Their skirmish could be an all-out brawl with a voice only they can hear, telling them to quit in the heat of competition. It always happens at some point in our training, when countless hours of preparation have already been logged, but there are countless more to go. Lost in a sea of endlessness, motivation can wane and the universal question each of us wrestles with looms big: "Why am I doing this?" Yes, even the greats in sport must answer that one!

Whatever the circumstance, whatever the source, a struggle is always temporary. A champion's experience teaches them this. They can take a quick look back and see that every struggle was washed aside when they allowed ease to take over: when the answer to a question came by quieting the noise of the struggle; when they changed course to be more effective and fluid; one with less tussle that led to the greater goal they were pursuing.

The champion in all of us can resurface unscathed by embracing the moment of encounter where our will clashes with reality. Avoiding it will likely bring it back bigger and stronger farther down the road. Take the struggle and neutralize it with the knowledge that it may be a part of the journey but it's not the whole of it. Soak in that thought and let it turn back on the ease and proficiency necessary to move through the moment at hand.

LET OTHERS MASTER THE KNOWLEDGE OF YOUR SPORT: A CHAMPION ONLY NEED MASTER ITS APPLICATION.

Sports are simple on the outside. There's a finish line and you have to get there. There's a ball and it has to go through the hoop, into the cup, across the goal line, and you as the vehicle of momentum must make that simple task happen. Repetition of your basic task makes a successful outcome more likely. Being the best, being your best, is much more complicated.

There are so many systems involved with coordinating your specific sport's requirements. Train the nervous system to be quicker and more efficient at delivering the impulses to working muscles that must fire just right. Strengthen the muscles themselves so they generate more force in the same mission. Fuel the body precisely so that every cell has the nutrients to work at optimal levels. Find and utilize the most progressive equipment of your trade. Get your mind in the sweet spot between relaxed and alert to allow your absolute peak level of performance.

Those are tall tasks to try to maximize. Knowing enough about any one of them is a profession in itself. That's why athletes hire coaches, have trainers, seek out psychologists, and travel with mechanics and equipment experts to the big show.

But while top levels require the guidance and support of specialists, the Art that makes a champion resides in the individual who can take that precious knowledge and master its application. Think of it this way. A sleep expert may be able to tell you that you need 7-9 hours each night to recover from your workouts, but it is up to you to know exactly where in that range "optimal" is for you. A nutritionist can explain how your sport demands you eat 1-1.5 grams of protein each day per kilo of body weight to recover properly, but it's up to you to sense where in that spectrum the right total for your body is on any give day.

A champion is a master at taking the most effective components of each expert's knowledge and passing it through the test of fire—training and competition—until the right chemistry results. Then and only then can performance reach genetic maximum levels. Champions let others master the knowledge of their sport. It's the champion's job to blend it all into a masterpiece using their skill and learned experience as a competitor.

GREATNESS BEGINS ONCE THE BATTLE IS DONE.

Every sport, every profession, has those who have achieved levels of excellence that live on in people's memories long after the competition is over. Winning streaks that stretch beyond possibility, improbable and inspiring comebacks against insurmountable odds, new standards that break barriers long considered unbreakable . . . these can all be put in the category of great.

But "great" and "greatness" are very different. A great moment is about the event. Greatness is broader. It includes the character of the individual who achieved the success that set a standard. "Greatness" is accomplishment wrapped in humility, achieved by a person who understands their time in the sun was a gift given, not a right earned. Greatness is taking the skill and the will that got them there and sharing it with others to in turn help them with their dreams rather than hording it away for personal use.

Greatness doesn't have to be anything that is public or newsworthy either. It's not reserved only for those who win. It becomes part of anyone's life who has tried, struggled, and then tried some more until they achieved a personal breakthrough, even if that standard of excellence was simply to take part as a competitor and to finish.

We are all like diamonds in the making. Situations of intense pressure allow something personal and deep to take shape and sparkle within our character, places that would otherwise have remained a lump of coal had we not gone through the test. Greatness, then, starts to take shape once the battle is done; the nugget is refined over time to expose its deepest beauty.

Greatness can be a stronger sense of self, one that washes away limiting images and thoughts. It can be a giant leap forward that is understood to be a part of life, not the reason for living. Greatness is being able to stand side by side with those who've tried but failed, without an ounce of gloat. It's refining the ability to stand tall and be proud of one's effort, even if the final outcome fell well short of the dream. Greatness is taking care of a precious moment, one forged through competition that gets passed around the park so that it becomes everyone's property and makes life richer.

OVER PREPARE AND UNDER TRAIN.

This particular quote might sound like a call to go in two completely unrelated directions to get ready for the moments that count most. But it's not! They are two great partners, necessary for bringing out your best when it's called for.

The groundwork that allows for your best to emerge at peak moments must be broad. Building such a solid foundation requires going beyond the field of play. The "over prepare" work comes by taking the extra steps beyond the basics of your sport to

be able to help make the demands of high level performance feel more like a normal act rather than something superhuman. It could be functional strength work, flexibility training, or seeking terrain and conditions more challenging than the day of competition demands. It's jumping higher, bounding farther, short bursts of speed that are faster, enduring bouts that are longer, all to take you beyond what is needed. Only then can excellence be touched with an ease and grace that makes it look, oh, so easy!

Over prepare is also the internal work that helps focus energy, quiet internal doubt and achieve the ability to lean on steadiness to carry you through the impossible moments of a quest. It's gaining the vision of how you will say, "I can." when your body is screaming "I can't." It's being equipped with a steadfastness that will take that final step into excellence no matter how difficult it is or how far it will stretch your abilities.

What will allow you to cross that divide separating good from great is having a reserve, an untapped reservoir of energy that a champion saves for the moment when excellence is defined. This is the Art in the quote. Prepare, but don't suck the well dry by over-testing your limits in the low payback environment of training. Art takes shape when "under trained" finally gets its chance, when the utmost effort has been held at bay and begs to surface, when the reservoir of possibility is finally accessed and greatness is unleashed at the most potent moment of competition.

PAIN IS THE SONG OF THE WORKING BODY. INTENSE PAIN IS ITS SYMPHONY. ENJOY THE MUSIC.

This was the first quote that came to me for the book, so in some ways it's my favorite. It triggered the solidification of so many lessons learned through competition and helped each take a form that can convert struggle into ease, challenge into one of the richest experiences available, and Competition into Art. The call in this quote is to work with your perspective on what is happening. On a very basic level we all know how important our view of a situation is to the experience of it. On days when training flows and your energy is high, you usually put the outcome of the day in the great category. If however, you do the exact same training session and you feel off, it can be logged away as a very frustrating and almost worthless effort. Both likely had the same amount of actual physical discomfort and challenge, but one was met with enthusiasm, the other with resistance. Clearly the same thing viewed from two different perspectives can have two very different complexions.

In the world of endurance athletics, working at a high level comes with its share of discomfort. But that's not bad! It's just a byproduct of your body functioning at peak capacity. It then becomes a choice of looking at it as either negative or as something positive. In fact most who become endurance sport champions don't consider a workout or a race their best unless it does come with a fair amount of body signals that a less trained person would view as negative. Champions enjoy the music.

Art happens by making this switch from viewing pain, challenge, pressure and expectation as something bad or unnerving to simply embracing it as a sign that you are in the midst of something great and incredible that is unfolding.

A symphony played by a myriad of instruments blends the sound of each into something sweet and moving as long as everyone is in key and on beat. Athletic performance is no different. When all the "instruments" of your body are in tune and on beat, your athletic symphony soars. Changing resistance to acceptance, making the shift from trying to avoid the "sound" of the working body to enjoying it, is what will realign your effort with your greatest potential. It brings every muscle fiber and thought back onto the same beat so that your "symphony" becomes a masterpiece.

IMPOSSIBLE IS A GREAT VICTORY TAKING SHAPE.

Preparation has one vast purpose: improve the predictability of an outcome and reduce the amount of wildcard influences that put lethal kinks in the best of plans. When all goes well it's impressive to say the least, especially in world-class athletics. But impressive does not necessarily cross over into Art, to a finish or outcome that's the stuff of legends. Runaway victories get a mention. Come-from-behind victories make headlines. The difference is when a level of impossibility enters the equation, when the fluency gained through training has a hard time understanding the language of the moment. Then it can seem that there's no answer to the equation being presented. It's not the impossibility that makes the day, though. It's the place of excellence one must go to in order to come up with an impossible solution that is capable of elevating the outcome to "unforgettable."

And there's a very simple reason why that is stratospheric in dimension. Going where you have never been called before takes something special. It is only possible when doubt is shelved, fear is tossed to the side of the road, and you leap with no regard for the safety or certainty of the landing. The grand scale of the challenge at hand is irrelevant. Impossible for one may be simple for another. But facing the impossible regardless of its scope is what turns a challenge into something great.

There is always a choice. Rise up and stay fully engaged with the impossible, or bow down to uncertainty. Which will you choose? Which would a champion choose? Staying in it doesn't guarantee the ending will be rosy. But that's what is absolutely required if a great victory is the goal.

REGROUPING IS NOT GIVING UP.

Staying the course and applying steady force with a singular focus can move mountains. A constant, fast pace can wear down even the steeliest of competitors. Getting even a slight lead, then continuing to outpace a worthy adversary, can eventually erode their will to match your standard. But what if you are the recipient of that unyielding force? What if it's your will that's about to crack into a million unrecognizable pieces? What's going to make your next step seem worthwhile when all you are seeing is an opponent who just seems to toy with you?

Are you going to just give up? You might! You've probably already looked at every option to try to turn things back in your favor, but only see dead-end possibilities.

Throwing in the towel can seem like the only way out. What can you do? This quote gives the answer. Regroup!

Back off ever so slightly and gather your forces. Let your worthy opponent continue to expend their energy. Take a break from trying even if it's as short as one or two breaths. Take in just a little more air and let out every bit of struggle. Regroup. It takes the pressure off the hopelessness of the moment and clears your mind. It erases the need to be in the lead and opens the doorway that guards the energy you need to relaunch with renewed possibility.

Regrouping is not giving up! Giving up is listening to: "I'm too weak; I don't have what it takes; I can't do it." Regrouping changes that channel! Stepping back for even a second can be enough to gain the energy needed to complete what you are so close to doing. It's tough to find that one-ounce extra you need when it's getting squeezed between "I want to quit" and "It's just not worth it." It will never come close to gaining traction if you give up! Take that breath. Drop back for a second. Regroup. Then re-engage with the force of a champion taking their performance to the level of Art.

THE REAL WORLD DOESN'T CARE ABOUT YOUR IDEAL STRATEGY: IT IS BEGGING YOU TO FOLLOW ITS PLAN.

Sometimes when we talk about "ideal," it's really code for "easy." It's an image we have in our minds that everything will go according to our plans. It doesn't necessarily mean that the journey will be without challenge, but we assume we'll be able to rise up and handle each eventuality that comes along the way. "Ideal" anticipates that the final result will always be what we set out to accomplish, done in the time we had in mind, and achieved in a fashion that suits us.

Here's the reality, though. If you have been alive for more than a few years, you are acutely aware that the real world rarely cooperates with our ideal. Is that unfortunate? Absolutely not! In fact, the real-world plan that we end up following usually gives us experiences that are priceless, that are much more grand than the ideal plan. Here's one story about this from my racing.

I had a clear goal to win the Ironman in Hawaii. Five years into that journey I had scraped the outer borders of that rarified objective, but never penetrated its sanctified core. Each of those same five years, one cement-solid competitor had been crowned the champion. Most of those victories came by snatching the lead from my grasp at the inevitable moment when I faltered. His name was Dave Scott.

In 1988 this fierce rival pulled out of the Ironman two days before it took place because of an injury that prevented him from being able to run. I looked at the start list. I had beaten everyone remaining. It would finally be my day, even if it would be sort of a default victory without Scott's participation.

The real world stepped in though. I got two flat tires early in the bike ride. I only had one spare. The time lost on the side of the road waiting for the support vehicle was more than I could make up. Devastated and feeling like I was cursed, I almost gave up the dream. Six Ironmans, six races within sight of victory, but I still had nothing to show for it. It had me wondering if I should just hang up the dream.

Fortunately I didn't. The next year's Ironman in Hawaii, my seventh, became one of the greatest races the sport has ever seen. Dave and I battled side by side for over eight hours in a race that covers 140.6 total miles in one single day. He came up a scant 58-seconds short of victory. His string of titles ended. My string started.

For years I had hunted that race. I had been cynical at times, thinking that I should have won earlier. I asked myself why I had to go through so much disappointment; my ideal would have been to win long before it actually happened. But the real world was begging me to follow its plan. And in the end the script was perfect. The crown was passed in a race where both my toughest competitor and I shattered the world's record. The tension of racing side by side with the best, for all but the final moments before pulling away for victory, became a watershed of emotion for all who watched. It showed that indeed the real world had a great plan in mind!

USE PRESSURE TO FOCUS ENERGY.

This quote probably seems pretty self-explanatory at first glance. It looks like a call to use the pressure of a situation to get you dialed in, and from there let the initial buildup of expectation and anticipation propel you beyond your normal. Use the pressure of a competition to help you gain an edge that you would have to work hard to get in a training session; let yourself get pumped up for the big game; take in the cheers of the crowd to help you outsprint a more talented competitor. From whatever realm you feel the pressure, use it to your advantage. Simple? Usually not! If it were, no one would buckle in the most critical and pivotal moments of sport or in life.

The key word in this quote is "focus," much more than "pressure" or "energy." Focus helps us concentrate the quality of our actions and direct them with a sharpness that cuts through barriers to reach excellence. The challenge is to use pressure to focus energy rather than have it be something that diffuses it.

That scattering happens when pressure gets mixed in with a lethal dose of negatives.

The paradox is that pressure usually comes because there is a suggested downside. We feel pressure at work in the form of deadlines, because our livelihood could be on the ropes if we miss them. Pressure in a sports environment can feel extreme for similarly negative reasons. In the harshest terms, there will only be one who is crowned champion! The negatives create the pressure. The Art is getting them balanced out with some positives that maybe you never thought about as relating to pressure, positives that can help focus your energies.

What are some of those? How about uncertainty? The overly negative could see uncertainty as a downside. The positive is that it means there exists incredible possibility to discover a level you never dreamed of. What about feeling like you might be completely unable to find any self-confidence when things get tough? The positive of that is that, yes, you may be thrust into a zone that is so foreign and uncomfortable that the only option seems to be to give in. But by doing that you could discover capabilities that would never have surfaced in your normal controlled approach.

The list goes on. But the message is simple. Pressure is the ultimate catalyst for engaging fully with what is required of excellence. Let that simple thought pervade your performance and help you focus your energy in just the right way for the moment at hand.

THOUGHT PRECEDES FORM; SILENCE PRECEDES PERFECT FORM.

Several quotes in this book have silence and quiet as a central theme. There's a reason. Thoughts take energy to sustain, and if they are not positive, their impact can influence the outcome of the day very differently than we want them to. Everyone has felt the mass that negative thoughts can bear. We may have been searching for self-confidence, but only found self-doubt, and with that, the test of competition just got tougher. Thoughts aren't all bad though! A positive one can be exactly what sparks the initial steps to doing something great in life. "I want to . . ." Whatever it was, that first thought got you moving; it created action. You put on your sneakers and hit the road! Then seeing the changes in fitness from repeatedly doing that simple act creates even more positive thought, which fuels the engine even further.

Analyzing thoughts help keep us on track and stay focused on our goals and dreams. Whether its building a successful business or becoming a world class athlete, analyzing progress can keep the road ahead straight, necessitating only minor adjustments in our strategy as it interacts with that very unpredictable environment called the real world. Thinking and analyzing helps us get within sniffing distance of the top level we aim for, the perfection we are after.

That final step, however, rarely takes place in a moment of great thought or analysis. Perfection resides just outside that neighborhood. The championship shot cannot be made if the player is thinking about winning at the moment the ball is released. Silence allows the act itself to take over. The solution to an impossible comeback will never present itself through analysis. That extra something that has never before taken form can only filter down when the competitor finds silence. Only then will that athlete understand what one-of-a-kind action is needed to achieve perfect form.

THE RIGHT ANSWER COMES BY ASKING THE RIGHT QUESTION.

In 1989, seven years into my triathlon career, I had zero victories at the most important race in the sport. Six attempts to have a great race at the Ironman in Hawaii had ended with no crowns. Of course there will only be one champion, so that leaves a whole lot of athletes off the list of victors over the years, but I felt like I had what it took. I just needed to grasp the secret, bring it out; but, how?

I'd consulted with experts in swimming, cycling and running. I had physiologists advising me on training. Nutrition experts were attempting to help with my race day nutrition, which is a critical key to an event that takes over eight hours to complete. I tried to emulate those who had won. They'd figured it out: just be a little more like them! Maybe if I could adopt their race day composure, it would lead me to victory as well. But nothing was cutting the mustard. I was being haunted by one of the harshest sports mottos at the time that said, "Second place is the first loser." That was me. I was at a crossroads. Six Hawaiian Ironmans, no championship wins. At what point do you just say, it's not in the cards? But that was not the right question! Asking whether I should give up on the dream was not going to bring the performance of a lifetime. I'd asked how to get faster, get fast enough to pull it all off on the exact day that every other competitor in the world was going to execute their own mind-bending performance.

I could best the rest at every other event across the globe. I could outpace the guy who set the standard year after year in Kona, as long as we raced anywhere other than at the Ironman on the Big Island of Hawaii. By that measure, it seemed to signal that my dream was indeed within the realm of reality.

Finally in the winter of 1989, just as I was starting to put in the initial groundwork for another journey to the Ironman, I came up with the right question.

"What is holding me back from the success I am after?"

It's such a simple question, isn't it? There's nothing technical, mysterious or hard to understand about it. But the answers that came transformed everything and put me in the sights of victory. Part of it was my training. I saw that I was indeed shying away from a handful of key workouts that would get me physically ready to deal with the demands of an eight-hour race in the heat and humidity of the tropics.

Another part of it had to do with something that was tough to admit. I was afraid of the race! How can you win a race that you are afraid of?

That was what I had to figure out. I simply replicated the parts of the day that made me shrink back. Heat. I trained in it. Wind. I trained in it. Dave Scott the guy to beat. I just imagined myself next to him, free of concern for his seemingly impenetrable ability. And the Island? When I went there I just asked that I could feel at ease. Those were the right answers that helped me be my best. And they came by asking the right question.

THE GREATEST VICTORIES CAN'T BE SEEN.

In 1968 I became inspired watching the Mexico City Olympics, especially the long-distance swimmers. They simply amazed me. I could barely make it across a 25-yard pool once. The Olympians could swim from one end of the pool to the other over and over. That was it! I had to give it a try myself.

So swim I did. For twelve years I trained and competed, with little to show for it in the way of titles or records. I was outstandingly mediocre at the sport. But I loved it, and I loved the camaraderie with my teammates. I should say I loved the training. It was a physical puzzle, working day in and day out to gain a few extra seconds per hundred.

The part I did not like was the competition. You see, I had a character flaw that I could not overcome. I could do fairly well if I was in the lead during a race. But the instant a worthy adversary started to gain a few inches on me I would either fall back just because I felt I couldn't beat them, or I'd tighten up giving it a try and my stroke mechanics would completely fall apart. Either way I ended up with the same result: I'd lose. These losses were very apparent. I choked in the clutch moments where others would find a way to rise up. It would not be until my first triathlon years later that victory over this unnerving pattern would change.

That event happened in 1982 in San Diego. It was a few months after seeing the Ironman on television and being called to that arena by something deep inside. Amazingly, in that race I started the run, the third and final leg of the event, in fourth place. Unfortunately for me, fifth was just seconds behind. He passed me after about a mile of running, and then the swimming tape started to play in my head. It said something like, "He's passed me and is pulling away, therefore he will end up in fourth, and I will finish in fifth place at best." But then another thought took over. "Yes, he did pass me, but maybe, just maybe, I can hold on and pass him back!" He'd gained a few seconds on me while I was having this conversation with myself, and I had to work hard, but slowly I started to reclaim my lost ground, then went on the offensive and pulled away from him!

I ended the day in fourth place, with the first three ahead of me being some of the best in the world at the time. On the outside what looked so amazing was that the three in front of me already had names in the sport. Everyone including me saw some potential as a triathlete far beyond what I had been able to do as a swimmer. But the greatest victory on that day was defeating the old tape that said, once you get passed, it's lights out—no chance of redemption. It was a victory that no one ever saw, but one that served me well years later in races all over the planet. The greatest victories can't be seen!

THERE IS NO SACRIFICE IN PURSUITS OF THE HEART.

During my career racing triathlons, people would ask me about the sacrifices I must be making to race. They would look at me with a deeply concerned expression on their face, the kind that said they were feeling sorry for me for having to miss out on so much of life because I was dedicating my energies to being an athlete.

Indeed there were choices I made that could look like I was sacrificing. I would rarely stay up late at night. I usually said no to most things decadent when it came to what passed between tooth and gum on the way to my stomach. But was I sacrificing? Not from where I stood.

I was following a pursuit of the heart. It brought me a freedom and fulfillment that no diversion would grant. Contentment came from giving everything I had to my pursuit. I experienced it through dedication rather than decadence. My social time lasted for hours, but it wasn't at a tavern. It took place before dark with the best of friends, spending our time together on bike seats rather than barstools.

If what you are dedicating your efforts toward is tipping the scales in the direction of feeling like you're missing out, a very honest discussion must be had with yourself. It can be telling you that the day to day of your quest isn't what's true to your heart. That is a very precarious ledge to be walking along. The goal has to be reached to be able to look back and say, with both fists held high, that, yes, the journey was worth what you put into it.

Pursuits of the heart are very different. These journeys are fulfilling because of the day-to-day effort they require. Yes, they may necessitate giving up things that make it look like you are sacrificing. But the clarity of your focus is energizing and fulfilling because it is coming from a dream that called you. Pursuits of the heart stir something deep inside that takes precedent over other parts of life that even you may have looked at as essential before the dream took hold. But now you can think of nothing more gratifying or worthy to focus on than the pursuit of your heart.

THE ART OF COMPETITION

SELF-CONFIDENCE ELUDES THOSE WHO NEVER FACE FEAR.

If you speak with most athletes about what holds them back in their mindset, it almost always comes down to something that relates to fear. It could be fear of another competitor's strength or fear of a weakness in their own makeup. On performance day that list can be long: fear of missing a shot, of not being able to handle the tough moments, of falling from an apparatus or slipping into an outlook that erodes the will to keep pace with the challenge at hand.

The opposite of all that is what we search for: to know we will be able to draw on our strengths when the road gets bumpy. We all want to know we can count on that place inside that will step up and fire the booster rockets when competition get tough. Art comes when you see that the something extra you need, call it self-confidence or going beyond the ordinary to gain the extraordinary, resides in the same place as fear. Both are deep. Both are powerful. Self-confidence cannot work its magic if fear is ignored.

Self-confidence is easy to feel in the calm of your living room. You can hold onto it when the scales of competition are tipped in your favor. It's much tougher to access when chaos takes over, and the scene in front of you has impossible slapped all over it. What's the solution? Start with your pre-competition prep. Look at every situation that could make your palms sweat. Figure out how you're going to climb out of those holes before the day comes when you might actually need to. See every weakness you have then know what your work-around solution is going to be. For every crack in the road, there's a way to jump across it.

Now you have faced your fear. Self-confidence is waiting. It's ready to provide you with the fuel and the skill to make every challenge a turning point.

It will be there for the first test of the day. It will be there in the next moment when another challenge pulls into sight. You now have self-confidence that can handle it all because fear will not grab hold; you've already faced it. It's a potent effectiveness that simply allows you to get the job done, no matter what shape that solution takes. You have gained a self-confidence that is always present when you stop thinking and allow full engagement to mark the day.

YOU ARE HALFWAY THERE WHEN THE JOURNEY IS NINETY PERCENT COMPLETE.

At the Ironman Triathlon in Hawaii there is a famous stretch of road called Ali'i Drive. It's the final march to the event's finish, leading from the barren lava fields where the majority of the race takes place to a corridor lined with thousands of fans cheering the athletes in. It's perhaps the most welcomed sight to everyone trying to cover 104.6 total miles of swimming, cycling and running all in one day. It signals they are so very close to completing their journey. Ironically, this celebrated length of dead-flat roadway is where some of the greatest meltdowns in Ironman history have taken place. Race leaders have been passed on this historic slice of pavement, one athlete crumbling to the ground as another takes the crown. It's amazing that athletes who have covered all but this final stretch to the watering hole can go from running to walking to crawling within sight of the finish banner. How can that be? What makes that last small percent of such a long day become the place where some of the greatest drama the Ironman has ever seen takes place? The answer? You are halfway there when the journey is ninety percent complete! The final stretch of any endeavor can be the toughest to hold on for. The finish can be in sight. The job almost done, but it still must be completed. The present has been bought, but it still needs to be wrapped. The playoffs have been won but the championship still waits. You go through some of the toughest wind and heat imaginable during an Ironman day, but the final stretch must be covered to collect the finisher's medal.

We dose our energies for the big events in life based on the size we see our goal to be from start to finish, so that at the end we know we have given it our all. The catch here is that the higher we set the bar, the greater the chance is going to be that the immensity of our journey will expand beyond any size we imagined it would be. Perhaps a great opponent threw something your way that you never thought possible. It could be that you are not functioning at your ideal level, yet the goal is not going to bend down low to accommodate. You must still rise up to its standard.

We often try to break our journey down into smaller pieces, thinking of the first half as the uphill and the second as the downhill when we can cruise, on momentum alone, to the finish. Rarely does it pan out like that. More often than not it's like climbing an arduously long trail up a mountain side, one that takes nearly all your effort just to get within sight of the summit, at which point its pitch doubles in steepness. You are halfway there when the journey is ninety percent complete!

There is a simple tool that can help you dose your energies, your enthusiasm, so that you become the master of that final ten percent, the toughest half of your journey. Place your finish line a quarter mile past that of your opponents. Convince yourself that you will cross theirs and keep running until you reach your finish that lays a few steps beyond. If you are two points down with a minute to go, don't aim for three. Make four or five points your goal and convince yourself that only with those five will you walk away the champion. If making up ten seconds a mile will catch the leader before the finish, make fifteen the goal and live its demand. Then the final ten percent of your journey will be your domain unfolding as Art in your favor.

265

EPILOGUE

Insight has many names: experience, knowledge, skill, expertise, understanding, even wisdom. It arrives bit by bit, distilled down into something potent and usable over a long period of time. It gathers from a vast base of seemingly insignificant events and focuses their essence into that very practical point where something incredible is sparked. It hints of its arrival through something you recognize immediately. You win. You overcome. You create something inspiring that triggers excitement and passion in others.

But that is not the insight. That is simply the event or the instant when every cell in your body resonates with the singular knowledge that something distinctive and exceptional just happened. It then becomes your mission to figure out what allowed grace to prevail and enabled you to enter the territory called Art.

Twelve years after my final Ironman victory, I was still trying to find the precise words that fully explained the internal shift that took me from zero Ironman victories to one and then, eventually, six. It was the sum total of that journey from struggle to triumph, to the final impossible conquest as an aging veteran of the sport that painted the full and complete picture of my career. People wanted to know the mindset that made that all possible. They wanted a chunk of my knowledge to give them that same chance to reign supreme over their Ironman challenges.

I thought about it, a lot. How did I win? I wasn't always a winner. It came by doing more than just training diligently. What was the grounding point that allowed me to pivot all that hard work into victory? Clearly a portion of that success hinged on mindset. Triumph in my races was achieved partly by outlasting the other competitors and certainly by out pacing the lesser qualities in my own character that would have me give up rather than endure pain or suffering in the pursuit of something important. But no matter what my answer to others was, I could tell my replies weren't giving them the full picture, one that would enable them to go out and create the extraordinary in their own pursuits. You would think if I could win six Ironman World Championships, I could then relate the experience full and exposed for others to savor and employ effectively.

I had a strong sense of what I was trying to say, but the right words were elusive. They were like fleeting glimpses so close I could see them out of the corner of my eye, yet the second I turned to grab their form, they were gone. But that's exactly why I knew I had to keep trying. Things we can describe easily are rarely the ones with impact. It's the indefinable traits in life–those that penetrate fear, skepticism and doubt, those that raise self-confidence or exert a powerful calm–that change your chances in an instant.

Insight can take its sweet time to filter down through our mesh of understanding until it finally touches a nerve that finally grasps it. That "Aha!" moment was about to come for me like a flood. It happened during a retreat I was on in Japan with Brant Secunda in the fall of 2007. It was twelve years almost to the day after my farewell victory in Kona. For two weeks we journeyed to many of the sacred places Japan has preserved for its people to contemplate life. In every area we entered, we would find others already there, on pilgrimage, leaving their offerings, asking for insight and a strong connection to all things sacred.

We had been there for about a week, the midpoint of our time together in that stunning land, with waterfalls, lakes, bamboo forests and temples so ancient they barely peer out from the cover of trees that have grown up and around them. The next day we would be going to one of the most sacred places in Japan: Mt. Fuji. Many consider it to be the embodiment of nature. I was resting on my futon bed in the hotel the afternoon before not really thinking about anything, just feeling the calm that pervades everything in Japan's countryside. And then the first insight floated in seemingly out of the ethers of awareness:

"PAIN IS THE SONG OF THE WORKING BODY. INTENSE PAIN IS ITS SYMPHONY. ENJOY THE MUSIC"

Then the next one followed a few moments later:

"THE GREATEST VICTORIES CAN'T BE SEEN."

They started lining up. Quote after quote seemed to be falling from the sky. I was there on a futon, catching each one with all the places in my being that had tried unsuccessfully for over a decade to express that rarefied state that allows you to race perfectly regardless of the chaos around you or the improbability of matching your prescribed measure of success. In a matter of a few hours time, I had nearly fifty quotes that seemed to reach the depths of what I had been searching for twelve years to fully convey.

I read them. I reread them. Each one took me to that place of possibility where the only thing that exists is the expansiveness your own potential creates when it is untethered from negative thoughts, where outcome is secondary to expression and great action is begging to be unleashed. It's a place I was forced to go to thousands of times in my racing when I wanted to quit. It was the place of one thousand-one where doubt is no longer allowed, where impossibility turns to background noise, then falls silent. It's the regrouping that enables full engagement unchained from thoughts of failure. It is that place where Competition turns to Art.

Insight that is explainable rarely reveals itself when we are trying to call it forward. Usually it divulges its secret code when we are daydreaming with no real thought about trying to find answers or solutions. Einstein commented that many of his greatest insights came while he was riding a bike. Those kernels didn't come at the chalkboard; they came to him during the rhythmic pedaling of a bicycle.

I was front and center in that universal place of daydreaming that afternoon in Japan. I was basking in the peace and inspiration I felt while spending time in Japan's nature preserves. I was filled with that expansive internal place of peace Brant brings us to during his retreats. The combination allowed the flow of words that finally captured how Competition can turn to Art. They formed the backbone of what you have read.

This book was created for you to help accelerate your journey to greatness and elevate all outcomes to Art, that place you may have seen glimmers of but also had a tough time describing to others. Hopefully some or all or maybe just one key quote, one completely inspiring photo, has taken you to that place within yourself where the only possibility is indeed that anything is possible! That is the Art of Competition.

MARK ALLEN

EPILOGUE

ADDITIONAL RESOURCES AND INFORMATION:

Brant and Mark teach retreats worldwide, titled Fit Soul, Fit Body, designed to bring many of the themes in this book alive. For more information and a listing of upcoming retreats go to:
WWW.FITSOUL-FITBODY.COM

They also co-authored an award-winning book titled **Fit Soul, Fit Body: 9 Keys to a Healthier, Happier You.** To purchase the book go to Amazon.com or contact your local bookseller.

Brant continues to share the Huichol tradition and principles for personal growth through ceremonies and retreats around the world. For more information on these life transforming events go to:
WWW.SHAMANISM.COM

Mark shares his principles of success in the corporate environment as well. For information on booking Mark at your next important conference go to:
WWW.MARKALLENSPEAKING.COM

If you are interested in getting ready to compete in a triathlon yourself, check out Mark's coaching website. It is currently offered in four languages and is being used by athletes in over fifty countries:
WWW.MARKALLENONLINE.COM

To learn more about Nick Borelli and his photography go to:
WWW.BORELLIPHOTOGRAPHY.COM

Photo page 80 courtesy of Nico Secunda
WWW.NICOSECUNDA.COM

Graphic design and layout by Jeff Keil
WWW.BEHANCE.NET/JEFFKEIL

THE ART OF COMPETITION

BIO: MARK ALLEN

No triathlete has gained the recognition or success that Mark Allen has. After competing and losing in the Ironman Triathlon World Championships in his first six attempts at this demanding race, he emerged victorious in 1989, winning the most difficult one-day sporting event in the world.

It would be the first of six Ironman victories for Allen, the last coming in 1995 at age 37, making him the oldest champion ever at that time. He also excelled at the Olympic distance, winning the sport's inaugural Olympic Distance World Championships in 1989 in Avignon, France. He went undefeated in ten trips to the Nice International Triathlon, and from 1988-1990 he put together a winning streak of twenty consecutive victories.

Over the course of a fifteen-year racing career, which ended in 1996, Mark maintained a 90% average in top-three finishes. He was named "Triathlete of the Year" six times by *Triathlete Magazine*, and in 1997 *Outside Magazine* called him "The World's Fittest Man". His most recent sports accolade came in November of 2012 when he was voted "The Greatest Endurance Athlete Of All Time" in a worldwide poll conducted by ESPN.

Since retiring from competition Mark shares his stories of Ironman racing with corporate audiences throughout the country, has a triathlon coaching service used in over fifty countries worldwide, and is an award winning author along with Brant Secunda for their award winning book *Fit Soul, Fit Body: 9 Keys to a Healthier, Happier You*.

BIO: NICK BORELLI

Nick Borelli's work honors our ever changing planet while incorporating subtle movement to enhance the amazing world we live in. Growing up in Santa Cruz, CA, Nick was always fascinated by waves and surfing and began photographing them for publication after returning home from The University of Massachusetts Amherst.

Knowing there was so much more to photograph, and through the guidance of great teachers and mentors, he moved his focus into earth's wildness and internal components of the landscape that make up the whole.

"As I look at a landscape, I try to capture broad views to express vastness, but also concentrate on little pieces that make the earth so special. I explore various angles and wait for light to explode the color and contrast various shade of black and white. My hope is to bring the viewer to a beautiful, peaceful place." Nick Borelli

THE ART OF COMPETITION

MARK ALLEN: 6X IRONMAN CHAMPION
PHOTOGRAPHY: NICK BORELLI